"Dr. Akin has provided a mu
groom but also a story abou
of Songs shows us how marriage ought to be neglecting neither
covenant nor passion. The words 'Christ-Centered' prepare us
for content where Jesus is the hero. The feature of each chapter,
'How does this text exalt Christ?,' keeps us looking for the gospel
story deep in Old Testament narrative. Truly a rich, practical tool
for pastors and teachers."

Kathy Ferguson Litton
National Consultant for Ministry to Pastor's Wives
North American Mission Board

"Very few can communicate the endless truths of the Song of
Songs as Danny Akin does. Not only does he help us to understand
this beautiful book from a biblical and expositional perspective,
he also relates it powerfully to the culture in which we live. I am
grateful that such a man with such incredible credentials has
given us the gift of this commentary. Thank you, Danny Akin.
We who love the Word in general and this book in particular are
indebted to you for your magnificent work."

Thom S. Rainer
President and CEO
LifeWay Christian Resources

CHRIST-CENTERED

Exposition

AUTHOR Daniel L. Akin
SERIES EDITORS David Platt, Daniel L. Akin, and Tony Merida

CHRIST-CENTERED
Exposition

EXALTING JESUS IN

SONG OF SONGS

HOLMAN
REFERENCE

NASHVILLE, TENNESSEE

Christ-Centered Exposition Commentary: Exalting Jesus in Song of Songs

© Copyright 2015 by Daniel L. Akin

B&H Publishing Group
Nashville, Tennessee
All rights reserved.

ISBN 978-0-8054-9676-5

Dewey Decimal Classification: 220.7
Subject Heading: BIBLE. O.T. SONG OF SONGS—COMMENTARIES\JESUS CHRIST

Printed in the United States of America
1 2 3 4 5 6 7 8 9 10 • 20 19 18 17 16 15
BethP

SERIES DEDICATION

Dedicated to Adrian Rogers and John Piper. They have taught us to love the gospel of Jesus Christ, to preach the Bible as the inerrant Word of God, to pastor the church for which our Savior died, and to have a passion to see all nations gladly worship the Lamb.

—David Platt, Tony Merida, and Danny Akin
March 2013

TABLE OF CONTENTS

ACKNOWLEDGMENTS

I would like to thank Shane Shaddix, Mary Jo Haselton, and Kim Humphrey, each of whom made significant contributions to this volume. You all have blessed and enriched my life.

SERIES INTRODUCTION

Augustine said, "Where Scripture speaks, God speaks." The editors of the Christ-Centered Exposition Commentary series believe that where God speaks, the pastor must speak. God speaks through His written Word. We must speak from that Word. We believe the Bible is God breathed, authoritative, inerrant, sufficient, understandable, necessary, and timeless. We also affirm that the Bible is a Christ-centered book; that is, it contains a unified story of redemptive history of which Jesus is the hero. Because of this Christ-centered trajectory that runs from Genesis 1 through Revelation 22, we believe the Bible has a corresponding global-missions thrust. From beginning to end, we see God's mission as one of making worshipers of Christ from every tribe and tongue worked out through this redemptive drama in Scripture. To that end we must preach the Word.

In addition to these distinct convictions, the Christ-Centered Exposition Commentary series has some distinguishing characteristics. First, this series seeks to display exegetical accuracy. What the Bible says is what we want to say. While not every volume in the series will be a verse-by-verse commentary, we nevertheless desire to handle the text carefully and explain it rightly. Those who teach and preach bear the heavy responsibility of saying what God has said in His Word and declaring what God has done in Christ. We desire to handle God's Word faithfully, knowing that we must give an account for how we have fulfilled this holy calling (Jas 3:1).

Second, the Christ-Centered Exposition Commentary series has pastors in view. While we hope others will read this series, such as parents, teachers, small-group leaders, and student ministers, we desire to provide a commentary busy pastors will use for weekly preparation of biblically faithful and gospel-saturated sermons. This series is not academic in nature. Our aim is to present a readable and pastoral style of commentaries. We believe this aim will serve the church of the Lord Jesus Christ.

Third, we want the Christ-Centered Exposition Commentary series to be known for the inclusion of helpful illustrations and theologically driven applications. Many commentaries offer no help in illustrations, and few offer any kind of help in application. Often those that do offer illustrative material and application unfortunately give little serious attention to the text. While giving ourselves primarily to explanation, we also hope to serve readers by providing inspiring and illuminating illustrations coupled with timely and timeless application.

Finally, as the name suggests, the editors seek to exalt Jesus from every book of the Bible. In saying this, we are not commending wild allegory or fanciful typology. We certainly believe we must be constrained to the meaning intended by the divine Author Himself, the Holy Spirit of God. However, we also believe the Bible has a messianic focus, and our hope is that the individual authors will exalt Christ from particular texts. Luke 24:25-27,44-47 and John 5:39,46 inform both our hermeneutics and our homiletics. Not every author will do this the same way or have the same degree of Christ-centered emphasis. That is fine with us. We believe faithful exposition that is Christ centered is not monolithic. We do believe, however, that we must read the whole Bible as Christian Scripture. Therefore, our aim is both to honor the historical particularity of each biblical passage and to highlight its intrinsic connection to the Redeemer.

The editors are indebted to the contributors of each volume. The reader will detect a unique style from each writer, and we celebrate these unique gifts and traits. While distinctive in their approaches, the authors share a common characteristic in that they are pastoral theologians. They love the church, and they regularly preach and teach God's Word to God's people. Further, many of these contributors are younger voices. We think these new, fresh voices can serve the church well, especially among a rising generation that has the task of proclaiming the Word of Christ and the Christ of the Word to the lost world.

We hope and pray this series will serve the body of Christ well in these ways until our Savior returns in glory. If it does, we will have succeeded in our assignment.

David Platt
Daniel L. Akin
Tony Merida
Series Editors
February 2013

Song of Songs

How to Begin a Divine Love Story

SONG OF SONGS 1:1-4

Main Idea: The Song of Songs paints a picture of marital love that reflects the love that instructs us in God's good design and points us to our faithful Shepherd-King, Jesus.

I. **Being Passionate for Your Mate Is a Good Thing (1:1-3).**
   A. What do you feel about your mate (1:1-3)?
   B. What do others say about your mate (1:3)?
II. **Desiring Intimacy with Your Mate Is a Good Thing (1:4).**
   A. Do you enjoy spending time with your mate?
   B. Do you value your mate for who he or she is?

The second-century rabbi Akiba ben Joseph said, "All the ages are not worth the day on which the Song of Songs was given to Israel; for all the Writings are holy, but the Song of Songs is the Holy of Holies" (Danby, *Mishnah*, 782). The rabbi was talking about a book we find in the Bible called "The Song of Solomon" or "The Song of Songs," an eight-chapter, 117-verse love song.

Few books have fascinated humans more than this one. God is never mentioned directly, if at all, in this book (but see 8:6). In this regard it is like the book of Esther. It also is never quoted directly in either of the Old or New Testaments. Its Latin title is "Canticles," which means "songs." It was one of the five megilloth (meaning scrolls) read annually by the Hebrew people at Passover (along with Ruth, Esther, Ecclesiastes, and Lamentations). It was penned by King Solomon, Israel's wisest king, who reigned ca. 971–931 BC over the united kingdoms of Israel and Judah. First Kings 4:32 says, "Solomon composed 3,000 proverbs, and his songs numbered 1,005." Yet of all the songs he wrote, the Song of Songs was his best.

A couple of major questions confront us as we prepare to mine this treasure trove of divine truth. First, how do we interpret this love poem? Second, how do we explain Solomon as the author of a song that extols marital monogamy and fidelity when 1 Kings 11:3 says, "He had 700 wives who were princesses and 300 concubines, and they turned his

3

heart away from the LORD." Let's take these two questions in reverse order, starting with the question of Solomon's promiscuous lifestyle.

Some believe the book is *about* Solomon or *written to* Solomon. On this view he is not the author. It may even be a critique of his sinful decisions in the area of marriage. Others believe Solomon wrote Song of Songs as a young man, his contribution to Proverbs as a middle age man, and Ecclesiastes as an old man. If this is true, and it is certainly possible, then Song of Songs is historical poetry about his first and truest love. However, I think it more likely that Solomon penned Song of Songs (probably later in life) as the ideal, as a poetic picture of what God intended marriage to be. It could even be a song of confession and repentance for his sins of adultery and polygamy. If this is true, then the song looks back to Genesis 1–2 and the beautiful love, harmony, and joy Adam and Eve experienced before sin entered the world and messed up everything (cf. Gen 3). It also anticipates the redeemed marriage relationship depicted in Ephesians 5:21-33. Douglas O'Donnell sums up well what I think is going on:

> The Song is a song that Adam could have sung in the garden when Eve arose miraculously from his side; and it remains a song that we can and should sing in the bedroom, the church and the marketplace of ideas. (*Song*, 20)

This understanding of the Song, I believe, helps us answer the first question: How should we interpret the Song? This clarity comes from understanding that Song of Songs is not a random collection of Syrian, Egyptian, or Canaanite cultic liturgies. It is not a drama with various acts or scenes, attractive as this view is. Nor is it an anthology of disconnected songs praising the bliss of human sexual love between a man and woman. There is unity and even progression in the Song too obvious to ignore. No, it is best understood as a theological and lyrical masterpiece that shows what marriage ought to be. However, and this is important, we must not stop with the natural reading of the text. We should complete the interpretive process and recognize that, as poetry, the Song was intended to evoke multiple emotions, feelings, and understandings. By way of analogy, it is easy to see how the bride and bridegroom in this Song portray to us God and Israel, Christ and His church, the Savior and His people. Jim Hamilton points us in a good direction when he says, "The Song is about Israel's shepherd King, a descendant of David, who is treated as an ideal Israelite enjoying an ideal bride in a lush garden where the effects of the fall are reversed" ("Messianic," 331). And Dennis Kinlaw fleshes out even more fully where God, the divine author of the Bible, intended to take us:

> The use of the marriage metaphor to describe the relationship of God to his people is almost universal in Scripture. From the time that God chose Israel to be his own in the Sinai Desert, the covenant was pictured in terms of a marriage. Idolatry was equated with adultery (Exod 34:10-17). Yahweh is a jealous God. Monogamous marriage is the norm for depicting the covenant relationship throughout Scripture, climaxing with the Marriage Supper of the Lamb. God has chosen a bride.
>
> [However], we tend to review the covenant-marriage relationship as an example of how human, created, historical realities can be used analogically to explain eternal truths. Thus human marriage is the original referent, and the union of God with his people is seen as the union of a loving husband and wife. . . .
>
> In reality there is much in Scripture to suggest that we should reverse this line of thought. Otherwise the union of Christ with his bride is a good copy of a bad original. The reality is, as Bromiley insists, that earthly marriage, as it is now lived, is "a bad copy of a good original." The original referent is not human marriage. It is God's elect love, first to Israel and then to the church.
>
> If divine love is the pattern for marriage, then there must be something pedagogical and eschatological about marriage. It is an earthly institution that in itself images something greater than itself. (Kinlaw, "Song," 1208)

Kinlaw is right. This earthly institution and this Song point us to a Bridegroom-King whose name is Jesus, a bridegroom who "loved the church [His bride] and gave Himself for her" (Eph 5:25). It should not surprise us that the Song of Songs is messianic and christological. After all, Jesus Himself said of the Scriptures in John 5:39, "They testify about Me." This, then, would include the Song of Songs. It anticipates the joys of salvation realized when we enter the chambers of redemption provided by this King (Song 1:4).

So as we walk through this carefully crafted love poem, we will see how it addresses the gift of marriage as it was intended by our great God.

We will raise points of practical application so that we might more perfectly put into practice what we learn. But then we will conclude each study by asking, "What do I see, feel, hear, and glean about my King, the Lord Jesus, from this text?" This promises to be an exciting, instructive, and worshipful journey to be sure.

Being Passionate for Your Mate Is a Good Thing
SONG OF SONGS 1:1-3

Bernard of Clairvaux said of this song,

> It is not a melody that resounds abroad but [is] the very music
> of the heart; not a trilling on the lips but an inward pulsing of
> delight; a harmony not of voices but of wills. It is a tune you
> will not hear in the streets; these notes do not sound where
> crowds assemble; only the singer hears it and the one to whom
> he sings—the lover and the beloved. (Griffiths, *Song*, xxi)

Sex, marital intimacy, is a good gift from a great God. He is the one who came up with this fantastic idea and I think He was having a really good day when He did! In other words, God is *pro-sex* when we engage in the act as He designed it and we do it for His glory. Yes, the glory of God should be the goal of sex, the goal of marriage. John Piper is exactly right:

> The ultimate thing to see in the Bible about marriage is that
> it exists for God's glory. Most foundationally, marriage is the
> doing of God. Most ultimately, marriage is the display of God.
> It is designed by God to display His glory in a way that no
> other event or institution does. (*This Momentary Marriage*, 24)

One of the ways we display God's glory in marriage is by being passionate for our mate. This honors one of God's designs in marriage. Perhaps that is why Solomon called this his "finest song," the best of the best.

What Do You Feel about Your Mate? (Song 1:1-3)

Following the title, the woman speaks, asking that her king (1:4) would shower her with passionate kisses: "Oh, that he would kiss me with the kisses of his mouth!" Interestingly, the bride, whom we could call Shulammite (the feminine form of Solomon, 6:13), does the majority of the speaking in this Song (53%, compared to the man's 34%). Indeed, she has the first and the last word. This stands in contrast to another book of wisdom, the book of Proverbs. I like the perspective of O'Donnell who says,

> The book of Proverbs can be called "a book for boys." The word "son" is used over forty times; the word "daughter" is never used. "My son, stay away from that kind of girl, and don't marry this kind of girl. But marry and save yourself for that girl—Proverbs 31:10-31." That's how the book ends, quite intentionally, for Proverbs is a book for boys. The Song of Songs is a book for girls. And its message to girls is, "patience then passion" or "uncompromised purity now; unquenchable passion then." I'll put it this way: In Proverbs the young lad is told to take a cold shower. In the Song of Songs the young lassie is told to take a cold shower. (*Song*, 24)

Why is the young lady so drawn to this man? First, because his love is intoxicating; it "is more delightful than wine." His passionate and affectionate kisses are sweet and powerful. "They sweep me off my feet. They set my head to spinning and my heart racing," she would say. I have read,

> the passionate kiss (average length one minute) reveals a lot about your relationship. Considered even more intimate than sex, passionate smooching is one of the first things to go when spouses aren't getting along. (*Marriage Partnership*, 10)

Her delight is not just in his kisses (touch and taste), they are also in his fragrance (smell): "The fragrance of your perfume is intoxicating" (1:3). He tastes good and he smells good. Being extremely practical for a moment, we can say he brushed his teeth and used mouthwash. He took a bath (or shower!) and used soap (or body wash!). He then put on his best cologne with "anointing oils" (ESV) or "aromatic oils" (MSG). She feels good about this man because he takes the necessary time and steps to make himself attractive to her. He does not take her for granted. He pleases her and he pleasures her. He sets her free to be the aggressor, something many cultures seem to shy away from, but not the Holy Bible.

It is clear she feels like there is no man like this man. There is no king like this king. There is nothing wrong and everything right in what she feels. Her desires are not dirty. Sex is never sinful when it takes place God's way and for God's glory. In that context, she will wait until the time is right (see 2:7; 3:5; 8:4). He is worth waiting for and so is she! First Corinthians 6:19-20 reminds us,

Don't you know that your body is a sanctuary of the Holy Spirit who is in you, whom you have from God? You are not your own, for you were bought at a price. Therefore glorify God in your body.

Our bodies are sacred gifts from God that have been redeemed by the precious blood of Christ, our divine Bridegroom. They are gifts to be used. They are gifts to be treated with care. This is what this bride believes and how she feels about her groom.

What Do Others Say about Your Mate? (Song 1:3)

This bridegroom-king's kisses are better than choice wine. His smells are exhilarating, even intoxicating. His fame and reputation are without question and widely known. "Your name is perfume poured out" speaks to his character as a person. He is like an anointed king, he *is* the anointed king, who is adored by the young women.

A person is always more, much more, than mere physical appearance. Wise people, when dating or courting, will not just form an opinion or make a judgment of the person with whom they are involved. No, they will also seek out and listen to the counsel of family and friends. They will listen to public opinion. Is he honest? Does she possess a Christ-like spirit that is gentle and quiet (cf. 1 Pet 3:4)? Does he have a bad temper? Is she financially responsible? Is he a flirt? A playboy? Does she accept her God-given assignment to submit to and respect her husband (cf. Eph 5:21-24,33)? Does he take joy in loving her sacrificially (Eph 5:25ff) and working hard to understand her (1 Pet 3:7)?

We should carefully consider what others say about the person we date, and especially about the person we would consider marrying. We all have blind spots. Love can indeed be blind. We must not let our emotions override good decision making, even if it hurts. Shulammite knew this man was respected. He was known as a person of character and integrity. She was not only physically attracted to him, she could respect him. She could admire him.

Desiring Intimacy with Your Mate Is a Good Thing
SONG OF SONGS 1:4

The Bible knows nothing of casual sex because, in reality, there is no such thing. What is often called casual sex is always costly sex. Sexually transmitted diseases (STDs), unexpected pregnancy, and psychological and spiritual scars are just a few of the results. The price many pay is high because we have approached God's good gift of sex all too casually. Sexual attraction is inevitable. It is what God intended. However, unless we follow God's plan, we will miss out on His best and suffer the painful and tragic consequences of sin in the process.

The Song of Songs explains the purpose and place of sex as God designed it. When we make love the way God planned, we enjoy the security of a committed relationship, experience the joy of unreserved passion, and discover the courage to give ourselves completely to another in unhindered abandonment.

Sociologists, and marriage and family counselors, are now discovering that the most emotionally and physically satisfying sex is between committed partners, and that satisfaction from sex increases with sexual exclusivity (one partner only), emotional investment in the relationship, and a lasting horizon for the marriage. They are also discovering that marriage is an excellent tonic for both mental and physical health and that marriage is far superior to cohabitation in both areas (Elias, "Marriage," 6D).

Do You Enjoy Spending Time with Your Mate?

The woman longs to be alone with her man, and so she excitedly exclaims, "Take me with you—let us hurry." And where does she want to go? "May the king bring me into his chambers" (my translation). She loves being with this man, and she is looking forward with eager anticipation to the time when she can be with him in private, in the bedroom. She wants to freely give herself to him in this way because of the kind of man, the kind of king, he is! She wants to be alone and she has no fear!

How do we get to this place in courting? In marriage? While there are a number of ways to get at this question I found the following list especially helpful:

- Take one another seriously (but not too seriously).
- Nurture one another (Eph 5:29-30).
- Set up a problem-solving strategy.
- Be respectful and courteous at all times. Treat your mate like a good friend.
- Spend time with your spouse (both quality and quantity).
- Make room for intimacy and affection without pushing always for sex.

- Treat one another as equals, because you are.
- Be honest with one another; always speak the truth in love (Eph 4:15).
- Give your spouse practical and relational priority in all aspects of your life.
- Be slow to anger, slow to speak, and quick to listen (Jas 1:19).
- Do not let the sun go down on your anger (Eph 4:26).
- Never stop caring about pleasing your spouse (Phil 2:3-4).
- Seek unity and do not feel threatened by disagreement (Phil 2:2).
- Honor one another's rights and needs.
- Do not impose your will on the other. Be peaceful and kind and use persuasion, not coercion.
- Seek to be one another's best friend.
- Try to deal with facts rather than feelings.
- Minister to rather than manipulate one another.
- Put your spouse before all others, including the children, except for Christ.
- Honor God's structure for marriage (Eph 5:21-33).
- Be approachable, teachable, and correctable (even and especially by your spouse).
- Do not try to control everything; give room for your mate to honestly express his or her feelings.
- Confront one another with tenderness, compassion, and loving concern, working hard not to frustrate your mate.
- Be willing to sacrifice for your loved ones.
- Do not neglect your responsibility to provide for your mate.
- Again, be willing to communicate and to listen!
- Despise divorce and determine it will never be an option.
- Eat as many meals with one another as possible.
- Whenever possible, postpone doing things you want to do for yourself to the times when your spouse is busy with other things.
- Do not stop trying to make time for your spouse just because it seems impossible to do so.

Do You Value Your Mate for Who He or She Is?

In the latter half of verse 4 a group of female singers, the daughters of Jerusalem, shows up (see 1:5). They have heard the words of Shulammite concerning the king and they wish to reinforce her opinion of this man: Your love merits praise and rejoicing. Because you so value this man, we value him too. More than that, we value who you are together! You prove the truth of Genesis 2:18: "Then the Lord God said, 'It is not good for the man to be alone. I will make a helper as his complement.'" Such beautiful complementarity evokes rejoicing and gladness. It calls for praise of such a pure and precious love that is better than the choicest wine.

Shulammite affirms her friends' good opinion of Solomon. It is a blessing to read this book and to see something really important. Not only does this couple love each other, they also like each other. They not only want each other, they also delight in bragging on each other. When asked how you could tell if two people are married, an 8-year-old boy named Derek said, "Married people usually look happy to talk to other people." This is sad, but it is often true. A stroll through the Song of Songs reveals something altogether different. Here are two people who are happiest when they are talking to each other! They are aware that they are sinners saved by God's grace. But saved they are, and now they are part of a story written in heaven by a divine and cosmic romantic. Our Lord loves a good love story. Song of Songs says it is so. Golgotha's cross says it even louder!

Practical Applications from Song of Songs 1:1-4

The Song of Songs begins with expressions of love, desire, passion, and longing for intimacy. It also addresses issues of character and reputation. Let's set forth some True-or-False questions to explore our perspective on these issues. Our goal, as always, is to have the mind of Christ (Phil 2:5), to think God's thoughts after Him. Take the test with your boyfriend or girlfriend if you are not married, with your mate if you are. After answering each question, talk over your answers. Work hard at listening and understanding. Look for biblical guidance and insight as you proceed.

T or F   1. Sexual desire and passion for the opposite sex is a good, natural and God-given desire.

T or F   2. The Bible frowns upon any type of intoxication, including being intoxicated with passion for your mate.

T or F   3. When it comes to intimacy in marriage, it is wise to involve all five senses in the process (i.e. touch, taste, sound, scent, and sight).

T or F   4. You should pay little or no attention to the opinion of family or friends when choosing a mate. It is your decision.

T or F	5.	A happy honeymoon probably guarantees a happy and lasting marriage.
T or F	6.	Children are essential to a happy and fulfilling marriage.
T or F	7.	Sex is only for the young, not the old.
T or F	8.	Growing in friendship with your mate is a key to growing in your intimacy with him or her.
T or F	9.	Being a student of marriage is a key to growing in my marriage.
T or F	10.	Being a student of my mate is a key to growing in my marriage.
T or F	11.	There is wisdom in knowing the difference between my needs and my wants.
T or F	12.	It is not essential, even necessary, to praise your mate in public.
T or F	13.	I am honestly intoxicated with my love for Jesus.
T or F	14.	Who Jesus is and what He has done for me (His Name) strengthens and sustains me day by day.
T or F	15.	I long to be with Jesus in the intimate and private place where I can simply enjoy His presence.

How Does This Text Exalt Christ?

Have a Passion for Your King!

"Solomon's Finest Song" is literally Solomon's "Song of Songs." It is a superlative like "holy of holies," "vanity of vanities," "King of kings," or "Lord of lords." And yet in the best song ever there is no mention, at least directly, of God. Is there any way to make sense of this? I believe David Hubbard provides a helping hand when he writes,

> God's name is absent from the entire setting. But who would deny that his presence is strongly felt? From whom come such purity and passion? Whose creative touch can ignite hearts and bodies with such a capacity to bring unsullied delight to another? Who kindled the senses that savor every sight, touch, scent, taste, and sound of a loved one? Whose very character is comprised of the love that is the central subject of the Song? None of this is to allegorize either the minute details or the main sense of the book. It is about human love at its best. But behind it, above it, and through it, the Song, as part of the

divinely ordered repertoire of Scripture, is a paean of praise
to the Lord of creation who makes possible such exquisite
love and to the Lord of redemption who demonstrated love's
fullness on a cross. (Hubbard, *Ecclesiastes*, 273–74)

The word *king* appears throughout the Song of Songs. He is the one
with whom the bride wants to be alone while the crowds praise him (1:4).
He is the one she wishes to please (1:12) and also with whom to be on
public display as she celebrates her marriage to him (3:9,11; 8:5). He is
her king, the one she longs to captivate with her attractiveness and beauty
(7:5). This king is like no other. He restores what was lost in the garden
(Gen 3) and He points to a wedding day and a marriage that only eternity
will realize (Rev 19:7-10; 21:1-2). No wonder the bride loves Him so.

Just as we rightly long for and have passions for our spouse, we
should desire with even greater fervency this Bridegroom-King whose
attractiveness is indescribable, whose Name is above every name (Phil
2:9-11), and who is truly the desire of all nations (Hag 2:7 KJV). Marriage
was always intended to point to Christ and His church. The Song of
Songs places this truth front and center for our gaze and meditation.
And what will we see? I think it will be this:

The Song's words resonate within the verbal manifold of
scripture's corpus, and when you pay attention to those
resonances you see, beyond reasonable dispute, that the
depiction of human memory, desire, and sexual love in the
Song figures both the Lord's love for you and yours for him,
and does so in a way that helps us to see that our human
loves for one another are what they are because of their
participation in his for us and ours, reciprocally, for him.
(Griffiths, *Song*, 11)

Reflect and Discuss

1. How have you heard the Song of Songs taught in the past? How
   have you interpreted it?
2. Why is the Song of Songs in the Bible? How do we understand it as
   Christians?
3. Why is it important to remember that God created sex? How does
   the Song help us keep human sexuality in perspective?
4. Why is it helpful to consider what others say about our potential
   spouse? What qualities should we look for?

5. What does the Song teach about the purpose of sex as God intended it? Why should it only be between a man and a woman committed to one another in lifelong marriage?
6. Which of the list of 30 ways to develop intimacy are most helpful to you?
7. What does it show the world when a married couple truly enjoys spending time with one another? Why is this quality an important feature in a marriage?
8. Take the quiz in the "Practical Application" section. Which questions were hardest for you to answer? On which did you and your spouse disagree?
9. How does this passage point to Jesus?
10. What New Testament passages might correspond to the truths in this text?

When a Godly Girl Is Having a Bad Day, What's Her Godly Husband to Do?

SONG OF SONGS 1:5-8

Main Idea: Marriage in a fallen world will mean we all have bad days, but as those redeemed by Christ, we can and should respond to one another with the love and grace we have received in Him.

I. **A Woman of God Can Still Struggle with Her Appearance (1:5-6).**
   A. She must deal with being defensive (1:5-6).
   B. She must deal with being disappointed (1:6).
II. **A Woman of God Can Still Be Anxious about His Absence (1:7-8).**
   A. She can experience sorrow and shame (1:7).
   B. He can provide her with praise and protection (1:8).

I am often fond of saying that even a good woman who loves Jesus, her husband, and family can every now and then have a bad day. My wife, Charlotte, had to live in a male dormitory for 20-plus years with me and our four sons. She once told me she was convinced that boys do things a dog wouldn't do! Once in a while she would have a bad day, and the boys and I came up with a warning code to put each other on alert. We would simply say, "Momma has got that look in her eye!" That was all that needed to be said. One day I came home only to have all four sons meet me outside on the front porch. Immediately they informed me "the look" was back and that it was back big time. I quickly surveyed the situation, found their assessment correct, and then provided the important counsel they needed: "Every man for himself!" I told them that the best I could tell, mom needed to be left alone for several hours, so I was going to leave her alone and I suggested they do the same. I ended my sage wisdom by saying if they crossed her path and got into trouble that they should not call for me! I wasn't coming! We were all on our own!

Every marriage has its rewards and romance. It will also have its rough spots and reality checks. Two sinners saved by grace through Jesus Christ are still sinners. We are going to disappoint our mate. We are going to hurt our spouse. That is why we so desperately need Christ. That is why, for a husband, the Bible says, "Live with your wives with an

15

understanding of their weaker nature" (1 Pet 3:7). Unfortunately we often stop here and do not read the rest of the verse: "showing them honor as coheirs of the grace of life, so that your prayers will not be hindered." A husband must both understand and honor his wife.

In these verses Solomon highlights two realities to which a man must be especially sensitive when it comes to his wife. One is how she sees herself: her appearance. The other is when he is away: his absence. Both are tender spots in the heart of a woman. She is fragile and vulnerable in these areas. A godly, Christ-redeemed husband will exercise TLC as he works to understand her and then minister to her. The image of a shepherd-king suddenly appears in these verses. This is exactly what she needs. A role model for every man to emulate is before us: our Shepherd-King Jesus is foreshadowed for our meditation. Where He is there is rest and security, the very things a husband following in His footsteps will provide for his wife. Echoes of Revelation 7:15-17 can be heard in the distance.

A Woman of God Can Still Struggle with Her Appearance
SONG OF SONGS 1:5-6

Women are sensitive to their physical appearance, far more than a man, though some men are gaining ground in this area. Her sense of self-worth and even value can often be tied to how she sees herself.

These verses are different from what goes before and what will follow. There has definitely been a mood change. Further, the woman is not addressing her man but the "Daughters of Jerusalem." This is "girl talk." Shulammite is not an aggressive lover here. She is an insecure and apologetic female whose past has inflicted pain and left some scars. Every person comes into marriage with some baggage. Sometimes it is the baggage of a particular personality; sometimes it is the baggage of a particular past. Either way, the issues must be faced and addressed. Only then can one's mate better understand the person. Only then can God administer His healing grace.

She Must Deal with Being Defensive (Song 1:5-6)

The woman asserts her beauty or attractiveness, but she does so with some hesitation. Shulammite knows she possesses natural beauty. She believed that she was pretty and attractive, lovely and pleasing in appearance. She was sensitive to the fact that men are creatures of sight and that they are so often moved by what they see. She was confident he would like what he saw when he looked at her. Of herself she can say, "I am . . . lovely." However, there is a problem with which she struggles. A tan was not grand in Solomon's day. Women prized fair skin and the "indoor look." This would signify a more lofty social standing of the well-to-do city girl. In contrast, Shulammite was deeply suntanned and dark. She was a country girl who had been "gazed on," "looked upon" (ESV) negatively by both the sun of nature and the sons of her mother (possibly step-brothers) who forced her to labor in the vineyards. "She had been doubly burned, by the sun, and by her brothers' anger" (Gledhill, *Message*, 104). "The tents of Kedar" speaks of "the Bedouin tribes whose tents, made from the hair of the black goats so common among them, are a frequent sight on the fringes of the deserts" (Carr, *Song*, 78). "The curtains of Solomon" draw a different analogy. These curtains would be beautiful and valuable, of "exquisite craftsmanship. . . . She is both hardened by the elements and yet beautiful" (Garret, *Proverbs*, 387). There are pluses and minuses as she saw things, though the minuses appear to have the upper hand at the moment.

She Must Deal with Being Disappointed (Song 1:6)

Shulammite makes a plea, "Do not stare at me because I am dark." I know my dark, Semitic Mediterranean skin is even darker than normal. However, there is a reason for my situation. I worked hard to tend the vineyards in the field because of the harshness of my brothers. As a result, my own vineyard, my body, has been neglected. Unable to give the time, attention, and care I would have liked, my physical appearance, at least to my way of thinking, is less than the best. One easily senses her pain, her insecurity. Tom Gledhill expresses her self-perception well:

> Her vineyard represents everything that conveys her essential femininity. Her looks, her complexion, her dress, her status, her sexuality—all those considerations which would make her attractive to a man. . . . In these verses we are brought face to face with the problems of our own self-image. How do we view ourselves? When we look at our own reflection in the mirror, do we like what we see? Can we accept ourselves as we really are, with all our quirks, idiosyncrasies and limitations? Do we like the way we look? Or are we always wishing we were like someone else? (Gledhill, *Message*, 105)

A woman's appearance is important to her. It requires on the part of a man great sensitivity and understanding. We will see her king respond with exactly what she needs in short order (see 1:8). He hears what she says and he knows how to respond! He meets her (and all of us) at our point of need.

A Woman of God Can Still Be Anxious about His Absence
SONG OF SONGS 1:7-8

Security is an essential element in a happy, healthy, and growing marriage. This is certainly true for a woman, especially if one of her specific "love languages" is time. For her, the beautiful four-letter word *love* is often best spelled as "T-I-M-E." Extended periods of separation are painful. It hurts. It confuses. But it can also motivate a woman into action! This is what Shulammite does.

The woman returns her attention to her man. However, she shifts the imagery from that of a king to that of a shepherd. Her man is a shepherd-king, one who pictures and anticipates the messianic Shepherd-King, the Lord Jesus Christ. What an incredible man he is! From the city to the country. From the palace of a king to the shepherd's tent. She wants to know where her man is and she does not want to ask for directions or consult a GPS!

She Can Experience Sorrow and Shame (Song 1:7)

With something of a teasing request, Shulammite expresses her desire to be reunited with her man with three complementary questions: "Tell me, you, the one I love: Where do you pasture your sheep? Where do you let them rest at noon? Why should I be like one who veils herself beside the flocks of your companions?"

Solomon is gone. Why that is, we are not told, though the imagery implies he is about the normal duties of life. Here the picture is of a shepherd tending his sheep. She misses him. She wants to be with him. To speak so frankly exposes her heart, but it will also excite the heart of her lover. At noon the sheep would sleep. The other shepherds would be resting. There would be time just for them. No distractions. No interruptions. A mid-day rendezvous! What a great idea! What a creative lady we see. Their meeting would be outside in the wide open spaces, perhaps under a shade tree, perhaps in a temporary hut or shelter. Even as she sorrows over his absence, she strategizes about how to make their intimate time together new, exciting, and memorable. But you can't love them if you're not with them. They need to rendezvous and get together, and they need to do it now.

To wear a veil as she wandered among the other flocks and shepherds would be embarrassing. It could, in that day, give the impression that she was a prostitute (see Gen 38:14-15) or that she was possibly in mourning. A prostitute has many men, but if they are absent, she has no man she can call her own. There is no one to whom she can point and say, "That man is my man." Shulammite did not want there to be the slightest doubt that Solomon was hers and she was his. For there to be even a question concerning their fidelity and commitment to each other would be shameful. Shulammite knew there was a cost, a price to be paid, in committing herself for a lifetime to another person, and she was more than willing to make the sacrifice.

He Can Provide Her with Praise and Protection (Song 1:8)

The man now speaks for the first time in the Song, and his words perfectly address both her concern of her appearance and his absence. First, he calls her beautiful, something he will do throughout the Song (1:8,15-16; 2:10,13; 4:1,7; 5:9; 6:1,4,10; 7:1,6). Second, he tells her where to find him. In essence he tells her to follow familiar paths or "tracks" that this shepherd-king is known to walk. Tremper Longman likens the scene to "a playful, sensual game of hide-and-seek" (*Song*, 101). I like that. His precise location is withheld, but a strategy for finding him is put before her. All of this draws our imagination to a romantic encounter far away from the public eye and the hustle and bustle of city life. This is the first time they steal a countryside getaway. It will not, however, be the last. Periodic times away and alone are a healthy tonic for marriage. This is a valuable lesson for all of us.

Practical Applications from Song of Songs 1:5-8

One of the ways to help your mate get over a bad day and to limit those bad days in the future is to work at communication. This is a theme we will see repeatedly in the Song of Songs because it is so important to a growing, healthy relationship. We need to be available. We need to talk. And this is crucial: we must cultivate the art of listening! Ours is more of a telling culture than a listening culture. We have to push back against its seduction. Below are ten suggestions to help keep open good lines of communication between a husband and wife. Walk through the list together, and then talk through what you each see individually as strengths and weaknesses. Work hard at listening to your spouse's perspective! It will be worth it.

1. Develop common interests. Start with the spiritual. Learn about each other's occupations and interests and try to put yourself mentally into your mate's situation to foster mutual understanding.
2. Sharpen your sensitivity radar. Observe your spouse for signs of satisfaction, frustration, happiness, weariness, etc., and react appropriately.
3. Learn to listen. Be intentional. Focus! Don't try to pry open a closed mind, but when your spouse voluntarily talks, listen attentively and intelligently.
4. Make yourself an interesting and desirable person. Keep mentally and physically fit and fresh so that you are magnetic to your mate. (And watch out for those tired late-night conversations!)
5. Avoid "sore spots" in conversation. Always approach "danger" areas with proper timing. Work at saying the *right thing* at the *right time* and in the *right way*.
6. Learn to accept criticism in a spirit of love and meekness. Try to examine yourself realistically from the viewpoint of your mate. Develop a teachable spirit.
7. Discuss problems with a willingness to settle for limited objectives (not having your way!), if necessary. Your overall relationship is more important than winning a temporary "victory." In this context, "compromise" is a good word.
8. Blend your recreational programs so that you can relax and "let off steam" together. Taking a 30-minute walk on a regular basis is an excellent strategy and habit.
9. As a wife, recognize that you need to siphon off tension. Work at being calm and cool-headed. As a husband, be decisive and reassuring in your love.
10. Take at least an annual time-out for a husband-wife "retreat" away from home. Evaluate the past and set goals for the future. Ask the Lord to help you learn from the past even as you plot a path for the future.

How Does This Text Exalt Christ?

The Security of Knowing My Shepherd-King

The theme, promise, and hope of a shepherd-king are rich and run through both testaments. It begins when the Lord called the youngest boy of a man named Jesse, his son named David (1 Sam 16–17). David was a shepherd who would slay Goliath, become Israel's greatest king, and receive a promise from God that he would have a descendant of whom God said, "I will establish the throne of his kingdom forever" (2 Sam 7:13). Later David would pen the beautiful Psalm 23, which speaks of the Lord as our Shepherd. Then in Ezekiel 34:22-23 the Lord promised His people, "I will save My flock, and they will no longer be prey for you. I will judge between one sheep and another. I will appoint over them a single shepherd, My servant David, and he will shepherd them. He will tend them himself and will be their shepherd." Finally, the Old Testament unfolding of this portrait reached its end in Micah 5:2,4, where we read of Messiah,

> *Bethlehem Ephrathah, you are small among the clans of Judah; One will come from you to be ruler over Israel for Me. His origin is from antiquity, from eternity. . . . He will stand and shepherd them in the strength of Yahweh, in the majestic name of Yahweh His God. They will live securely, for then His greatness will extend to the ends of the earth.*

Promise becomes fulfillment in Jesus, the Son of David, whom the Bible calls "the good Shepherd" in John 10:11, "the great Shepherd" in Hebrews 13:20, and "the chief Shepherd" in 1 Peter 5:4. In Revelation 7:17 we discover this Shepherd is "the Lamb who is at the center of the throne" who guides His people to "springs of living waters."

This glorious future Shepherd-King is anticipated in the bride-groom-shepherd-king of the Song of Songs. He is the One who pastures well His sheep and gives them rest. His presence banishes all fears and insecurities, for He has promised those who love Him, "I will never leave you or forsake you" (Heb 13:5; cf. Deut 31:6). We may draw near to this Shepherd-King and find protection, provision, security, and shade. First Peter 2:21 teaches us to follow in the steps, the tracks (Song 1:8), of the one who is "the Shepherd and Guardian of [our] souls" (1 Pet 2:25). Here in Song of Songs we find a faithful and loving Shepherd, a

Shepherd-King, whom the people can love, trust, draw near to, and follow. Here we find a shepherd-king who points us to Jesus.

Reflect and Discuss

1. Why is it wrong to think that because we are forgiven and redeemed in Christ, we can no longer have "bad days"?
2. Women, have you noticed yourself being particularly sensitive to your physical appearance? How does the Song instruct you to respond to this impulse?
3. How should a man respond when his wife is feeling especially insecure? Where can he look for guidance?
4. Why is time so important in a relationship? Does this change as our relationship moves ahead through the years?
5. Which of the suggestions for improving communication in a marriage is most difficult for you?
6. Which of these suggestions for improved communication have you found most helpful?
7. In what ways does this passage point us to Jesus?
8. How does Jesus show love and patience when His church is "having a bad day"?
9. How does Psalm 23 inform and enhance the shepherd portrait in the Song of Songs?
10. Why do you think the shepherd image is so prominent in the Bible?

There Is Power in Praising Your Spouse

SONG OF SONGS 1:9-14

Main Idea: Marital love that is transformed by redeeming grace will be filled with praise and encouragement for both spouses, reflecting the love Christ has shown us on the cross.

I. **Tell Her How Valuable She Is to You (1:9-11).**
   A. Tell her there is no one like her (1:9-10).
   B. Tell her no cost is too great to honor her (1:11).

II. **Tell Him How Special He Is to You (1:12-14).**
   A. Tell him you desire him (1:12).
   B. Tell him you love him (1:13).
   C. Tell him you need him (1:14).

A number of years ago I read a book that had a profound effect on my life as a husband and a father. The book is *The Gift of the Blessing* by Gary Smalley and John Trent. In it they provide both biblical and practical advice on how we can bless rather than curse the relationships of life, how we can build up rather than tear down those we love and care for. When it comes to our mate, their counsel is invaluable. They explain how God has put each of us together in such a way that we have emotional and physical needs that can only be met by acceptance of intrinsic worth, affirmation, encouragement, and unconditional love. We all have the desire and need to receive "the blessing" from others. "Others" include our heavenly Father, but it should also include our spouse. Neither is to be excluded if we are to receive true holistic blessings. They then point out that the essential elements of the blessing include five things:

1. *A meaningful touch.* This includes handholding, hugging, kissing, and all types of bodily contact that have the purpose of communicating love and affection.
2. *A spoken word.* This element can demonstrate love and a sense of worth by the time involved and the message(s) delivered. Its repetitive nature is crucial.

3. ***Expression of high value.*** This involves our passing along a message to others that affirms their intrinsic worth as a person. Praising them as valuable is the key idea.
4. ***Picturing a special future.*** This is the prophetic aspect of the blessing. What do our words tell others we believe the future holds for them? How do our present descriptions (nicknames) of others lay the foundation for future attitudes and actions on their part? How often it is that children, in particular, fulfill the earlier expectations and predictions of a parent and friends, for good or ill? Positive words of encouragement regarding future possibilities are those that will bless rather than curse.
5. ***An active commitment to see the blessing come to pass.*** This characteristic is both God-ward and man-ward. God-wardly, we are to commit others to His blessing and will. Man-wardly, we are personally to make the commitment to spend whatever time, energy, and resources are necessary to bless others.[1]

This list makes it clear that blessing our mate involves both words and actions. It includes what we *say* and what we *do*.

In Song of Songs 1:9-14 both words and actions are in view, but our words are especially emphasized. Solomon wants us to understand a vitally important truth when it comes to a healthy and growing marriage: there is power in praising your spouse. Words matter and they matter a lot. The Roman orator Cicero said, "We are all influenced by a desire of praise" ("Speech for Aulus," XI.26). Solomon would agree, and so he puts together two striking poems of admiration. The first (1:9-11) is spoken by the shepherd-king in praise of his lovely and much-valued lady. The second is voiced by the "most beautiful of women" (1:8) to her exceptional and much desired man (1:12-14). There is tremendous wisdom in these few verses. There are also some very interesting images and metaphors we will need to unpack. Be prepared to laugh and blush!

Tell Her How Valuable She Is to You
SONG OF SONGS 1:9-11

The scene shifts from verse 8 to verse 9. We move from the simple shepherd's field to the magnificent world of the Egyptian Pharaoh.

---

[1] See more developed explanations in Gary Smalley and John Trent, *The Gift of the Blessing* (Nashville: Thomas Nelson, 1993).

Solomon has been sensitive (see Eph 5:28-29) to Shulammite's insecurities concerning her appearance (Song 1:5-6) and his absence (v. 7). He addressed both of them in verse 8, telling her she is the "most beautiful of women" and also giving her guidance in how she can find him.

However, and this is important, he did not stop there. He continues to talk with her in verses 9-11 with words of praise that would bring joy to her heart and blessing to her soul. He wants her to know she is the best! There is no girl like his girl! No lady can compare to his lady!

As we walk through these verses there is something that we must not miss: the words and gifts of Solomon are genuine and from the heart. He is not trying to bribe her or buy her. He desires to bless her and to do so in a way that speaks to her heart. Solomon had learned, or was at least in the process of learning, to speak her "love language." Gary Chapman, in *The Five Love Languages*, points out that we all speak at least one of five love languages. Some are even equipped to speak several, and with varying dialects! However, it is rare that a husband and wife speak the same love language. After all, opposites do attract. Dr. Chapman identifies the five love languages as:

1. Words of Affirmation
2. Receiving Gifts
3. Acts of Service
4. Quality Time
5. Physical Touch

The following verses will leap with personal applications if we will keep this insight in mind. As a couple grows in their knowledge of one another, they will also learn to hear, understand, appreciate, show love to, and respond to one another.

Tell Her There Is No One Like Her (Song 1:9-10)

Solomon told Shulammite she was the "most beautiful of women" in verse 8. Now he calls her "my darling" (ESV, "my love"; REB, "my dearest"), something he will do repeatedly—nine times—throughout the Song (cf. 1:15; 2:2,10,13; 4:1,7; 5:2; 6:4). The word communicates to her his commitment and devotion, his delight and pleasure in her. Her step-brothers may have mistreated her (1:6), but he will honor her both in word and in action.

She is his darling and so he compares her "to a mare among Pharaoh's chariots." You have got to be kidding! Is he serious?! Yes he is, and she would have clearly understood and appreciated the compliment in the cultural context of that day. Pharaoh's chariot horses would have all been stallions. A mare would have been beautiful, noble, valued, and exceptional in their midst. She would have been a "black beauty" (cf. 1:5) that would have garnered the immediate attention of every stallion in sight! Now we see the compliment. She is like the one and only woman in a world of men, and she is a stunningly beautiful woman at that. She is priceless! No one is like her. She is a choice and valued bride.

In verse 10 Solomon focuses on certain specific features that cause her to stand out: "Your cheeks are beautiful with jewelry, your neck with its necklace." The bridles of Pharaoh's chariot horses were often adorned with beautiful jewelry and Solomon may still have the image of a stately mare in mind. This man notices the things that enhance her natural beauty, and he tells her what they are. These adornments do not make her beautiful, they complement her beauty. Tom Gledhill suggests, "Her rounded *cheeks* are enhanced by large circular *ear-rings* which emphasize the roundness of her face. Her neck is decorated by row upon row of strings of brightly colored beads. This enhances her height, her stateliness, as well as giving a slight hint of inaccessibility and protection" (Gledhill, *Message*, 112; emphasis in original). In Solomon's opinion, there is no one like her. No one compares. She has no equal. And he tells her so! There is power in his praise of his partner.

Tell Her No Cost Is Too Great to Honor Her (Song 1:11)

No price tag can be put on the one to whom God knits our hearts (cf. 8:6-7). Solomon will withhold no good thing from the one he loves. He will see to it that she is further honored with gold jewelry accented with silver. The most valued metals are not too good or costly to be showered on her. Richard Hess nails it: "Whatever the cost, he will honor her. The focus of his love has no limits as to the cost or task that he must undertake to bless her" (*Song*, 67).

My friend Matt Carter loves to talk to men about how they can "win" or "win back" the hearts of their wives. His counsel is good advice for any man, and it reflects the wisdom of these verses in the Song of Songs:

1. I will tame my tongue. When it comes to my wife, I need to be quick to listen, slow to speak, and slow to anger.
2. I will talk to my wife the way I would if a special and important person were visiting my home.

3. I will always be upbeat and positive in my interactions with my wife. I am not called to critique her. I am called to love and accept her.
4. I won't use my words to try to *take* from her. I will just give and bless, thinking about what she needs, not what I need.
5. I will strive to serve my wife every day.
6. I will win my wife's heart so she, in turn, will *want* to be mine.
7. Just as divorce is not an option with me, I want that same reality to be true for negativity or harshness with my wife. It is *not* an option for me to be harsh with my wife. Not under any circumstance. Ever.
8. I will sow seeds of righteousness by consistently committing to walk with the Lord. God will give me the power to bear this fruit and love my wife wholeheartedly. (McCoy and Carter, *Real Win*, 149–50)

Treat your wife in this way with your words and actions and she will know that she is valued by you. She will know she has won your heart, and she will be moved to give hers to you in response.

Tell Him How Special He Is to You
SONG OF SONGS 1:12-14

This woman knows that she is loved and valued by the man in her life. In word and action he has demonstrated his commitment and devotion to her. Now she returns the compliment without any fear or hesitation. Her confidence in his love for her frees her to love him in return with passion and sensual expressions of that love. The insecurities she felt in verses 5-8 have vanished. They have been vaporized by the love of her shepherd-king!

It is beautiful to watch the two lovers engage in a game of praise! This will go on for quite some time. What a wonderful contest for any couple to enter! Let's see who can out-praise the other! What a great way to bless and love your mate.

We must never forget a familiar but important nursery rhyme from the 1800s: "Sticks and stones may break my bones but names [or words] will never hurt me." That saying is not true. Words are indeed powerful weapons with the ability to bless or curse, heal or hurt. No wonder God's Word addresses the issue so often, especially in the Proverbs. Note just ten of many:

There is one who speaks rashly, like a piercing sword; but the tongue of the wise brings healing. (Prov 12:18)

The one who guards his mouth protects his life; the one who opens his lips invites his own ruin. (Prov 13:3)

A gentle answer turns away anger, but a harsh word stirs up wrath. (Prov 15:1)

The tongue that heals is a tree of life, but a devious tongue breaks the spirit. (Prov 15:4)

Pleasant words are a honeycomb; sweet to the taste and health to the body. (Prov 16:24)

Life and death are in the power of the tongue, and those who love it will eat its fruit. (Prov 18:21)

The one who guards his mouth and tongue keeps himself out of trouble. (Prov 21:23)

An endless dripping on a rainy day and a nagging wife are alike. (Prov 27:15)

Do you see a man who speaks too soon? There is more hope for a fool than for him. (Prov 29:20)

She [the virtuous wife] opens her mouth with wisdom and loving instruction is on her tongue. (Prov 31:26)

The woman of our Song is truly a Proverbs 31 lady. Let's listen in on how she speaks, in wisdom, to her lover.

Tell Him You Desire Him (Song 1:12)

Once again Shulammite addresses her lover as "the king." He is a shepherd-king, a bridegroom-king. The king "on his couch" or "at his table" indicates a time of rest and relaxation. It could also suggest the ideas of intimacy and lovemaking as they look forward to their wedding day (3:6-11) and their wedding night (4:1–5:1). She loves him and she wants to make love to him.

Appealing to his sense of smell, she says "my perfume releases its fragrance." The word for "perfume" is the rare word "nard." It will occur again in 4:13-14, and also in the anointing of Jesus for his burial (Mark

14:1-9; John 12:1-8). Nard, or spikenard, was an expensive fragrance. Hess informs us,

> Pure nard was a fragrance native to the Himalayan region of India. . . . Its scarcity and difficulty of manufacturing and transporting it a long distance made it both valuable and exotic. Perhaps this is the reason it is mentioned only three times in the Old Testament and only in the Song (4:13-14). As the most expensive of the perfumes mentioned, it also had the closest association with the king. Yet the female lover refers to it as "my nard." (Hess, *Song*, 69)

Carr adds that nard was in "much demand as a 'love-potion'" (*Song*, 85).

Shulammite is sexually aroused and seeks to elicit the same emotions in her man. And he is her king and he is worthy of a sensual and expensive display of affection. The release of her perfume and its fragrance creates an environment for lovemaking and romance. He is precious to her and much valued. She will hold nothing back.

Tell Him You Love Him (Song 1:13)

Tremper Longman notes,

> This verse stretched the imagination of allegorical interpreters with its explicit sensuality. Cyril of Alexandria is at his creative best when he suggests that the verse describes what we today would call biblical theology. The breasts are the Old and New Testaments, presumably only linked by their two-ness. Jesus Christ is the sachet of myrrh. The New Testament is in the Old concealed; the Old in the New revealed. Jesus spans the testaments as the sachet spans the woman's two breasts. (Longman, *Song*, 106)

The ancient allegorists did indeed stretch their imaginations with some of their interpretations. However, the woman of our Song had quite an imagination herself, and her love for her man frees her to express it.

Shulammite says, "My love is a sachet of myrrh to me, spending the night between my breasts." The overtones are both intimate and sexual, picturesque and yet chaste.

> Myrrh is a resinous gum gathered from a species of a South Arabian tree. . . . In liquid form it would be carried in small

> bottles like nard, but it was also used in solid form. This way
> it could be carried in a small cloth pouch or sachet and worn
> next to the body. . . . They myrrh was mixed with fat . . . as the
> fat melted from the body heat, the aroma of the myrrh . . .
> would fill the room. (Carr, *Song*, 85)

What Shulammite does here is moving. She compares her shepherd-king to this precious sweet-smelling bundle, one that lies all night between her breasts, close to her heart. "Her thoughts of him are as fragrant and refreshing as the perfume that rises before her. . . . She carries those fragrant thoughts of him through the night in peaceful sleep" (Glickman, "Song for Lovers," 37). Nestled between her breasts against her beating heart, there is an intimate bond of love, longing, and loyalty that cannot be broken. There is a connection, a commitment that virtually transcends words. All night long he laid his head as a precious fragrance between her breasts. She trusts him so completely, she loves him so dearly, she can make available to him the most intimate and precious parts of her body. She holds nothing back. She knows she does not need to.

Tell Him You Need Him (Song 1:14)

The woman now compares her man to a luscious and fruitful water garden, an oasis surrounded by desert. They have returned to the garden of Eden where the damaging effects of the fall are absent, nowhere in sight (see Gen 1–2). All is beautiful and fruitful. Death is outside in the desert. There is only life in this paradise for lovers.

Again Shulammite refers to Solomon as "My love." Theirs is an exclusive love relationship. He is a one-woman kind of man, and she is a one-man kind of woman. But she says more. He is refreshing, like "a cluster of henna blossoms to me, in the vineyards of En-gedi." The henna bush can reach a height of ten feet. It has thick yellow and white flowers in clusters and smells like roses. It is semitropical vegetation, and it grows at the En-gedi Oasis on the western shore of the Dead Sea, south of Jerusalem and just north of Masada. Longman notes, "Hidden and private, it is a romantic place to be sure" (*Song*, 106). The flowers, beautiful to see and sweet to smell, are a rare find in a desert's arid climate.

The analogy is striking. Solomon is like an oasis with its surprising pleasures and provisions in a desert. He is a rare find and therefore of inestimable value. It is as if the woman is saying, "All I have seen is a desert of men until I met you. You are my oasis with your beauty and fragrance. No man refreshed me until I met you. I dream about you. I think about you. I dream about us. I think about us. You are truly all I need. The very thought of you is a continual source of mental, physical, sensual, and spiritual pleasure. No man can make me feel like you make me feel." Here is passion that flows from praise. *Passion in the bedroom is always preceded by passion in all the other rooms.* Once again we see there is power in praising your spouse.

Practical Applications from Song of Songs 1:9-14

Abraham Lincoln said, "The success of a marriage depends not only on having the right partner, but on being the right partner" (McRae, *Preparing*, 86). Part of being the right mate is developing the art of praising your mate, loving her with your lips, "wowing" him with your words.

Steve Stephens says, "A healthy marriage is a safe haven from the tensions of everyday life. We need to hear positive things from our mate" ("37 Things," 177). He then shares 37 things we can and should say to our mate in order to bless, build up, encourage, and "wow" them! I love his list, and how I pray this will be the normal and regular vocabulary of marriages everywhere, beginning with mine! They prove beyond a shadow of a doubt there is power, awesome power, in praising our spouse.

1. "Good job!"
2. "You are wonderful."
3. "That was really great."
4. "You look gorgeous today."
5. "I don't feel complete without you."
6. "I appreciate all the things you've done for me all these years."
7. "You come first in my life, before kids, career, friends, anything."
8. "I'm glad I married you."
9. "You're the best friend I have."
10. "If I had to do it over again, I'd still marry you."
11. "I wanted you today."
12. "I missed you today."
13. "I couldn't get you out of my mind today."
14. "It's nice to wake up next to you."
15. "I will always love you."
16. "I love to see your eyes sparkle when you smile."
17. "As always, you look good today."

18. "I trust you."
19. "I can always count on you."
20. "You make me feel good."
21. "I'm so proud to be married to you."
22. "I'm sorry."
23. "I was wrong."
24. "What would you like?"
25. "What is on your mind?"
26. "Let me just listen."
27. "You are so special."
28. "I can't imagine life without you."
29. "I wish I were a better mate."
30. "What can I do to help?"
31. "Pray for me."
32. "I'm praying for you today."
33. "I prize every moment we spend together."
34. "Thank you for loving me."
35. "Thank you for accepting me."
36. "Thank you for being my spouse."
37. "You make every day brighter." (Stephens, "37 Things," 177–78)

How Does This Text Exalt Christ?

The Delights of Knowing My King

In Psalm 45 we discover a royal wedding song that is unique to the psalter. Its language echoes that of our Song in a number of places. Some even believe it was first written for Solomon and his wedding. Like the king of our Song, this king in Psalm 45 is praised by others (v. 1) and is the most handsome of men with grace flowing from his lips (v. 2). He loves righteousness and hates wickedness (v. 7). Myrrh, aloes, and cassia perfume his garments (v. 8), and he desires with passion the beauty of his bride (v. 11). And, concerning this king, God Himself says, "Your throne, God, is forever and ever" (v. 6); "I will cause your name to be remembered for all generations; therefore the peoples will praise you forever and ever" (v. 17).

Psalm 45 points to the same king as the Song of Songs. They are one and the same. He is the Messiah-King, the promised King, the One that Hebrews 1:8-9 informs us is Messiah Jesus. Of Psalm 45, Alexander MacLaren said, "Either we have here a piece of poetical exaggeration far beyond the limits of poetic license, or a greater than Solomon is here" (Boice, *Psalms*, 381). One greater than Solomon is portrayed in Psalm 45. One greater than Solomon is on display in the Song of Songs as well.

This great King has beautifully adorned His bride (Song 1:9-11) for her wedding day (Song 3:6-11; cf. Rev 21:2), and she, along with the Spirit, invites all to come and enjoy the pleasures provided by the Bridegroom (Rev 22:17). Whereas He has made her cheeks beautiful with jewelry (Song 1:10), He gave His own cheeks "to those who tore out His beard" (Isa 50:6) as our suffering Servant-King. And all that we lost in the fall, being banished from the lush waters of the garden of Eden, we now regain as our Lover takes us into the beautiful oasis of En-gedi. This King, Shepherd, Bridegroom, and Lover is Paradise restored, and more! The delights He has for us are greater than we could ever imagine.

The world in which we live is a desert place indeed. We will never find in it what we need for life. All it offers is thirst, destitution, longing, and death. But in Christ our Shepherd-King it is altogether different. Here is the water of life, beauty, rest, and everything you will ever need. He is an Oasis of life for all who flee to Him. Won't you come and rest in all He provides? Jesus said, "Come to Me, all of you who are weary and burdened, and I will give you rest" (Matt 11:28). What He says is true. Come and see!

Reflect and Discuss

1. What are some specific ways you can be a blessing to your spouse?
2. Why is it so important to *verbalize* praise for one's spouse?
3. How does Solomon show us the ways to praise one another?
4. How far would you go to honor your spouse? Does your answer reflect God's love for His bride?
5. Why is verse 13 so difficult to interpret? What are some options for how to explain the explicit detail?
6. What does it mean that these two lovers have "returned to the garden of Eden"? How does this idea fit into the book as a whole?
7. Why is "passion in the bedroom always preceded by passion in all the other rooms"? How can you show this latter passion?
8. What is the greatest praise you have received from your spouse? Why did that mean so much to you?
9. How do we understand that this text points to Christ?
10. Can you identify some themes that our text has in common with Psalm 45?

The Art of Intimacy

SONG OF SONGS 1:15–2:7

Main Idea: Physical and emotional intimacy are essentials in a marriage that reflects God's intended design because they show us the love and affection God has for His people in Christ.

I.   **Learn to Say the Right Thing (1:15–2:2).**
    A. Admire your mate's attractiveness (1:15-16).
    B. Appreciate your mate's thoughtfulness (1:16-17).
    C. Affirm your mate's uniqueness (2:1-2).
II. **Seek to Respond in the Right Way (2:3-6).**
    A. Tell him he makes you feel safe (2:3).
    B. Tell him he makes you feel loved (2:4-6).
III. **Determine to Wait for the Right Time (2:7).**
    A. Commit yourself to your God that you will wait.
    B. Commit yourself to your mate that you will wait.

Lasting romance and marital intimacy might well be put on the endangered species list in Western civilization in the early twenty-first century. On the one hand, cohabitation in the United States has increased by more than 1,500 percent in the past half century. In fact, more than half of all marriages are now preceded by cohabitation, even though evidence indicates that "couples who cohabitate before marriage (and especially before an engagement or an otherwise clear commitment) tend to be less satisfied with their marriage—and more likely to divorce—than couples who do not. Those negative outcomes are called the cohabitation effect" (Jay, "Downside").

On the other hand, we are seeing a rise in what some call "Grey Divorce," with there now being a significant number of persons divorcing after the age of 50. For the first time in our country's history, "more Americans 50 and older are divorced than widowed, and the number is growing" (Roberts, "Divorce"). Stephanie Coontz, speaking particularly for women, says that in our day, "if you are a healthy 65, you can expect another pretty healthy 20 years. So with the kids gone, it seems more burdensome to stay in a bad relationship, or even one that has grown stale. . . . We [women] expect to find equality, intimacy, friendship, fun, and even passion right into what people used to see as the 'twilight years'" (Roberts, "Divorce").

We read all of this and can draw only one clear conclusion: men and women have not changed since God put Adam and Eve in the garden in Genesis 2. Both are looking for and longing for a love that is real and a love that will last. Sin, unfortunately, has us looking for love in all the wrong places and often thinking about it in lots of wrong ways. Nevertheless, we cannot escape the reality that God said, "It is not good for the man to be alone, I will make him a helper as his complement" (Gen 2:18). As a result of the way God made us, we thirst for a love that is real and a love that will last. We pine for an intimacy that is the fruit of a love that truly is a gift from God. As James Russell Lowell said so beautifully in his poem "Love," we have an insatiable hunger for

A love that shall be new and fresh each hour,
As is the sunset's golden mystery,
Or the sweet coming of the evening-star,
Alike, and yet most unlike, every day,
And seeming ever best and fairest *now*.
    (Lowell, "Love," 22; emphasis in original)

In Song of Songs 1:15–2:7 we see the shepherd-king and his "darling" (1:15), the "most beautiful of women" (1:8), continue their "parade of praise" for each other. However, their dialogue quickens and intensifies. The expressions of their love for one another are even more direct and intimate. As Dennis Kinlaw well observes, "It hints of a return to Eden (Gen 2:18-25), with its simplicity, naiveté, equality, and purity. It is as if this were the original couple" ("Song," 1221). Yes, their intimacy and purity harks back to Eden, and it also looks forward to what a husband and wife regain and enjoy in Christ (Eph 5:21-33; Col 3:19-20). The alienation resulting from the curse that has marred and destroyed so many marriages is capable of being overcome through the gospel. Paradise regained and more again resounds in these verses. The act of intimacy is rediscovered in a bed lush with foliage (Song 1:16), a valley of beautiful flowers (2:1-2), a forest with apple trees (2:3), and a banquet hall filled with raisins, apples, and love (2:4-7). Once again we see our heavenly Father providing "good things to those who ask Him" (Matt 7:11).

Now what are some practical and specific steps we can take to cultivate a love that lasts and to excel in the art of intimacy?

Learn to Say the Right Thing
SONG OF SONGS 1:15–2:2

In our song the man is a shepherd-king, a lover who is "so idealized that he scarcely seems to touch the ground" (Webb, *Five Festal Garments*, 19). This is not surprising because this male human is a type of our divine-human lover, the Lord Jesus.

The woman is a lovely (1:5), beautiful lady (1:8) who is much valued by her man. One of the keys to a fulfilling and happy marriage has been captured early in their relationship: healthy and positive communication! We saw this in 1:9-14 and we see it continue in this passage of Scripture. Criticism and contempt, hangovers from the fall, are far removed from their relationship.

Steve Stephens is helpful at this point when he challenges couples to let "your speech always be gracious, seasoned with salt, so that you may know how you should answer each person" (Stephens, "27 Things," 175; see also Col 4:6). Stephens lists 27 things we should avoid saying to our mate: words that hurt, cut and tear apart. He says,

> There is nothing more painful than having unhealthy communication with the one you love. It is through communication that we connect and our spirits touch. If that connection becomes contaminated, it is only a matter of time before the whole relationship is poisoned. In the process of communication, wisdom is knowing what not to say rather than what to say. . . .
>
> Therefore, I gathered together some close friends and asked them what not to say to your spouse. Here is their list:
>
> 1. "I told you so."
> 2. "You're just like your mother."
> 3. "You're always in a bad mood."
> 4. "You just don't think."
> 5. "It's your fault."
> 6. "What's wrong with you?"
> 7. "All you ever do is complain."
> 8. "I can't do anything to please you."
> 9. "You get what you deserve."
> 10. "Why don't you ever listen to me?"
> 11. "Can't you be more responsible?"

12. "What were you thinking?"
13. "You're impossible!"
14. "I don't know why I put up with you."
15. "I can talk to you until I'm blue in the face and it doesn't do any good."
16. "I can do whatever I like."
17. "If you don't like it, you can just leave."
18. "Can't you do anything right?"
19. "That was stupid."
20. "All you ever do is think of yourself."
21. "If you really loved me, you'd do this."
22. "You're such a baby."
23. "Turnabout's fair play."
24. "You deserve a dose of your own medicine."
25. "What's your problem?"
26. "I can never understand you."
27. "Do you always have to be right?" (Stephens, "27 Things," 175–76)

Both Solomon and Shulammite knew the importance of words. They knew the power of words. Both were interested in fanning the flames of love with words of affirmation and blessing. Both were determined to develop and grow in the art of intimacy. Three particulars unfold for our consideration and edification.

Admire Your Mate's Attractiveness (Song 1:15-16)

Solomon again tells his lady she is beautiful (cf. 1:8). In fact he does it twice in verse 15. He will also do it later, on their wedding night (4:1,7). This is a gentle reminder to men that our wives appreciate repeated compliments. Once is obviously not enough. He truly and genuinely finds her attractive, and he tells her again and again. I like the striking nature of the CEV here: "Look at you—so beautiful, my dearest! Look at you—so beautiful!"

Solomon also again calls her "my darling" (cf. 1:9). The ASV translates the phrase as "my love." It is a term of intimacy and endearment. His heartfelt affection for her is strong. She is precious to him.

And he also says to her, "Your eyes are doves." As they look longingly and intensely into each other's eyes, Solomon speaks of her captivating eyes (see 4:9; 6:5; 7:5). The one who has the eyes of a dove is his dove (2:14; 5:2; 6:9). Lloyd Carr notes, "Beautiful eyes were a hallmark of

perfection in a woman. . . . Rabbinic tradition identifies beautiful eyes
with a beautiful personality" (Carr, *Song*, 86). This woman's eyes were a
barometer of her character, of the kind of godly lady she was. From the
outside or the inside, Solomon saw Shulammite for the radiantly beautiful lady that she was, and he told her so!

Appreciate Your Mate's Thoughtfulness (Song 1:16-17)

Shulammite now returns his compliment with one of her own. She is
especially appreciative of his thoughtfulness and attention to detail. She
begins by telling him she likes the way he looks too! He is handsome,
she loves him, and he is delightful. The word translated "handsome"
is the same Hebrew word as "beautiful" in verse 15, except it is in the
masculine gender. "The word occurs 14 times in the Song, but only this
once in the masculine form" (Carr, *Song*, 86). "My love" could be translated "my lover," a term of affection she has already used twice (1:13-14).
"Delightful" has the idea of pleasant or pleasing. He is all that she could
want in a man, and the economy of words she uses to express this is
quite remarkable.

As he was specific in his praise of her, she will be likewise in verses
16-17. First, she addresses the beauty of their bed. Second, she addresses
the beauty of their home. He is thinking of everything! Notice the word
our appears three times. These are the blessings of marriage they will
share together. The two have become one.

Their marriage bed will be sexually active and sensually attractive.
It is "lush with foliage"; alive, fresh, and fruitful. It is a perfect environment for passionate lovemaking that God heartily approves. And "the
beams of our house are cedars, and our rafters are cypresses" ("firs" or
"pines"). Their home is safe, secure, and sturdy.

Paul Griffiths says Solomon has built her a "magnificent home," a
"king's house." He also notes,

> These decorations are mentioned elsewhere in Scripture,
> where they belong to Solomon's Temple (1 Kgs 5–6) or to the
> palaces of the first kings of Israel. . . . Once again, the text
> pushes beyond its surface meaning and draws the attuned
> reader toward a deeper one, according to which the beloved
> [the beautiful woman] is in the temple, accepting and
> rejoicing in the Lord's caresses as do both the church and
> Israel. (Griffiths, *Song*, 48)

Affirm Your Mate's Uniqueness (Song 2:1-2)

There is an old hymn sung about Jesus that says, "He's the Lily of the Valley, the Bright and Morning Star; He's the fairest of ten thousand to my soul" (Fry, "Lily"). There is little doubt that song was based on Song of Songs 2:1. And there is no doubt the hymn is building on a misinterpretation of the verse. Christ is not the lily of the valley. The beautiful woman is, and by extension, we are!

Speaking of herself, Shulammite says she is "a rose [better, a common wildflower] of Sharon, a lily of the valleys." Hers is a natural beauty that promises fruitfulness and love. Richard Hess is particularly insightful at this point, making an interesting connection with other Scriptures:

> The female goes on to describe herself as the lotus [lily] of the valley (2:1). In parallel with the asphodel [rose of Sharon], it suggests fruitfulness but also beauty and love. As a lotus [lily] this term describes the decorations of the temple (1 Kings 7:19, 22, 26; 2 Chron. 4:5). In Hosea 14:6 (14:5 Eng.) Israel's blessing is likened to a blossoming lotus [lily] and a cedar of Lebanon. The Song's earlier images of trees compare with those of a flower in this verse; but in Hosea they describe the resurrection of a nation and its blessings of prosperity and well-being. Thus the self-description of a female lover (in Song 2:1) is one of self-confidence in which her beauty becomes a key to fruitfulness and success for the male. Here it seems that God has created the natural world primarily as a paradise in which the couple may find one another and enjoy their love. The nature imagery will continue throughout the book. Its intensity at this point allows the female lover to develop the thought of her partner and to present their love as a part of the natural world, which God created. In a similar vein Jesus compares the lotus or lily favorably to Solomon with all his splendor (Matt. 6:29). (Hess, *Song*, 75)

The shepherd-king is quick to respond to her modest expression of self-beauty. He again refers to her as his "darling" and he picks up on the image of the lily, carrying it to heights far beyond hers. You are unique, utterly remarkable, my darling. You are not just a flower among flowers, one *of* a million. No, you are one *in* a million, a beautiful wild flower among thorns. You are a flower that reminds me of Eden, and in comparison all other women are like thorns and conjure up images of the curse! You are like an only flower in a world of thorny weeds. That is what you are to me. You are different and distinct, separated in my eyes from all others. Your beauty outshines all others. They may be pretty flowers too, but when I compare them to you, they come up as thorns. Ours is truly a restored, redeemed relationship (Eph 5:21-33). Do you hear my words, my dear? Can you sense my heart, most beautiful of women?!

Seek to Respond in the Right Way
SONGS OF SONGS 2:3-6

Psalm 1 is a wisdom song that portrays the righteous man as a fruitful tree "whose leaf does not wither. Whatever he does prospers" (Ps 1:3). Perhaps Shulammite had this very psalm in mind when she responded in verses 3-6 to Solomon's words of kindness in 2:2. Ultimately Psalm 1 is fulfilled in the One greater than Solomon, the Lord Jesus (Matt 12:42; Luke 11:31). But Solomon, in our Song, typifies the One who is greater than he, and his bride-to-be finds him utterly delightful (2:3) with all that he provides for her. He shades her (2:3) and sustains her (2:5). He invites her into a house of love (2:4) and his loving embrace is an undeniable evidence of his devotion (2:6). He indeed "provides and cares for her, just as Christ does for the church" (Eph 5:29).

So she, as Tremper Longman says, "responds with a botanical analogy of her own" (Longman, *Songs*, 111). Every woman longs to have a man who is strong and reliable, dependable and trustworthy. This woman has found such a man, and she lets him know it. She also lets him know she wants him.

God has given us some biblical principles governing sex. Given that our text anticipates the issue, let's consider at this point some good guidelines given by our great God. How do we respond to our mate in the right way in this tender and sacred area of life?

1. Sexual relations within marriage are right, holy, and good. God encourages intimate union and even warns against its cessation (1 Cor 7:5).
2. Pleasure in sexual relations is both healthy and expected as we share our bodies with one another (Prov 5:15-19; 1 Cor 7:5).
3. The pursuit of sexual pleasure is to be guided by the principle that I will esteem the needs of my mate as more important than my own (Phil 2:3-4).

4. Sexual relations are to be regular and normal. No exact number of times per week is right or correct, but the biblical principle is that both parties are to provide adequate sexual satisfaction to their mate so that both "burning" (sexual desire) and temptation to find satisfaction elsewhere are avoided (1 Cor 7:9).

5. The principle of satisfaction means that each party is to provide sexual enjoyment as frequently as the other party requires. Other biblical principles (moderation, seeking to please another rather than oneself, etc.) also come into play. Consideration of one's mate always is to guide one's desires for sexual relations.

6. There is to be no sexual bargaining between married persons ("I'll not have relations unless you . . ."). Neither party has the right to make such bargains. This is a form of "marital prostitution" and must always be avoided.

7. Sexual relations are equal and reciprocal. The Bible does not give the man superior rights over the woman or the woman superior rights over the man. Mutual stimulation and mutual initiation of relations are encouraged in Scripture.

8. Whatever is safe, pleasing, enjoyable, and satisfying to both is acceptable. The *body* of each belongs to the others (1 Cor 7:4). Neither should ever demand from the other what is painful, harmful, degrading, or distasteful to him or her.

Tell Him He Makes You Feel Safe (Song 2:3)

This verse is specific and sensual as the imagery of God's good creation is again employed. Our beautiful lady compares her delightful man to an apple (or "apricot") tree found in the forest. This is who her love is "among the young men." An apricot or apple tree in the woods would be rare and something you would not expect to find. It would be attractive to the eyes and sweet to the taste. It also would provide needed sustenance. Solomon said she was a flower woman among thorny women. Shulammite says Solomon is a special tree amid ordinary woods. Finding him brought her great delight, and she loves "to sit in his shade." She delights in him. She is comforted by him. She is protected by him and only him. "I never knew love before, then came you" could be the song of Shulammite's heart.

Shulammite is secure and safe in Solomon's shade, his watchcare. She now longs for physical intimacy, for lovemaking and sexual union.

She simply says, "His fruit is sweet to my taste." The language is chaste and appropriate. It is not lewd or out of bounds. It is also highly suggestive and erotic. What I find in him I like. What I taste, smell, and feel is sweet and causes me to want more and more. Romance truly is an environment that prepares us for sexual union. As they anticipate their wedding night (4:1–5:1), the flames of passion are under control, but they are burning.

Tell Him He Makes You Feel Loved (Song 2:4-6)

Solomon brings Shulammite into "the banquet hall," literally "the house of wine." This is the only time this phrase is found in the Bible. Wine has already been associated with their love (1:2) and it will be again (4:10; 7:9). "He is intoxicated with her and has brought her to a place to make love" (Longman, *Song*, 111).

Yes, they desire a private time of sexual union, but their love is something Solomon wants the whole world to know. "He looked on me with love" could be translated "his banner over me was love." I like that rendering better. This is a reference to a military banner used in warfare to rally and gather the troops. The ideas are those of strength, protection, and identification. Her lover is not ashamed to declare his love for her in full public display. His intentions to make love are rooted in a love he is happy for all to see!

Shulammite is overcome by all of this. "I am lovesick" also could be rendered "I am faint with love." The "I" is emphatic. "Quick! Give me something to eat!" is her cry. "Sustain" and "refresh" are both imperatives. "Raisins," like "apricots" (apples), were viewed in that day as highly erotic and sensual. Sexual vibes are everywhere in the air.

In the passion of the moment, Shulammite is still aware of his gentle touch and his warm embrace (2:6). With one hand he cradles her head. With the other he lovingly holds and caresses her. Interestingly, the Hebrew word translated "embrace" is used in the Old Testament "both of a friendly greeting (Gen 48:10) and of a sexual union (Prov 5:20)" (Carr, *Song*, 93). He is her friend and her lover. Both are vitally important, especially to a woman.

Our beautiful bride has a king who extends his banner over her and who will provide for and protect her for the rest of her life. This reminds me of another King who has a bride He has promised to provide for and protect for all of eternity!

Determine to Wait for the Right Time
SONG OF SONGS 2:7

A number of years ago a sexual purity movement began called "True Love Waits," which challenged young men and women to make a pledge of sexual abstinence until they married. It is being renewed in our day as the "True Love Project." The new pledge, which focuses on the work of Christ and the pursuit of purity, reads,

> In light of who God is, what Christ has done for me, and who I am in Him, from this day forward I commit myself to Him in the lifelong pursuit of purity. By His grace, I will continually present myself to Him as a living sacrifice, holy and pleasing to God.[2]

Such a pledge clearly has biblical warrant. In fact it has a fan in the most sensual and sexual book in the entire Bible, Song of Songs. Not once, not twice, but three times we read in this love song, "Young women of Jerusalem, I charge you by the gazelles and the wild does of the field; do not stir up or awaken love until the appropriate time" (2:7; 3:5; 8:4). Let's unwrap this solemn oath that Shulammite lays on these young virgin women.

Commit Yourself to Your God That You Will Wait

This verse takes the form of an oath as Shulammite charges (ESV, "I adjure you") the young women of Jerusalem. "Give me your word," "Promise," "Swear to it" is the idea. But why mention "the gazelles and the wild does of the field"? Both are creations of God; beautiful female animals, vigorous and sexually active *in season*—the right time ordained by their Creator. And yet, something more subtle may be going on that you would only see (better "hear") in Hebrew. A number of Hebrew scholars have noticed that the Hebrew word for "gazelles" is *sebaoth*, which could suggest the name "Yahweh of *Sebaoth*" (the Lord of Hosts or Armies). And the Hebrew words for "wild does" are *ayeloth hassadeh*, which sound similar to "El-Shaddai" (Gledhill, *Message*, 128). This would be a creative and even playful way of evoking the divine names without

---

[2] From the "Commitment Card," accessed July 9, 2014, http://www.lifeway.com /Digital/True-Love-Waits/c/N-1z13u0lZ1z13wiu.

actually using them. Any Hebrew child would have immediately recognized the similarity in sound. The young women of Jerusalem would have done the same, and they would understand that it strengthened and raised the stakes of the oath they were being placed under.

Commit Yourself to Your Mate That You Will Wait

"Love should have its own rhythm and its proper progression. Too fast, too soon would spoil it all" (Kinlaw, "Song," 1222). This is a great word for singles, and this is the word that Shulammite has for the "young women of Jerusalem." "Do not stir up or awaken love until the appropriate time." *The Message* (MSG) says, "Don't excite love, don't stir it up, until the time is ripe—and you're ready."

Ecclesiastes 3:5 reminds us that there is "a time to embrace and a time to avoid embracing." Sexual relations are a good thing—a God thing—when they happen at the right place, with the right person, in the right way, and at the right time. Not just any time is a good time. There is a proper time, a God time, and it is called marriage. "Patience now, passion later. . . . So that's 2:7. Trust God's timing before marriage—wait for your spouse and your wedding day. Wait" (O'Donnell, *Song*, 61). I have never met anyone who said that they regretted waiting. I know way too many who regret that they didn't.

Practical Applications from Song of Songs 1:15–2:7

Sexual attraction is one thing, but marital intimacy is something different. The former can be almost immediate, but the latter grows over time. By God's grace, it grows deep over the years as we share life together. Below is a short and simple marital intimacy test. It is not complicated at all, but it could be insightful and helpful as you seek to grow closer in the intimacy department. A periodic checkup is good for our physical health. It is good when it comes to our marriages too!

A Marital Intimacy Test

(Answer: 4 – often, 3 – often enough, 2 – not enough, 1 – rarely, or 0 – never for each.)
Place the wife's score in the first blank; the husband's in the second. Then have a loving and healthy conversation concerning what you discovered.

1. How often do you show affection for each other that your mate truly appreciates? ___ ___

2. How often do you laugh at each other's jokes? ___ ___

3. How often do you say something nice and kind to each other? ___ ___

4. How often do you compliment your spouse in front of others? ___ ___

5. How often do you enjoy sexual intimacy? ___ ___

6. How often are you playful with each other? ___ ___

7. How often do you look each other in the eyes while talking? ___ ___

8. How often do you give each other a little surprise? ___ ___

9. How often do you say please? ___ ___

10. How often do you say I'm sorry? I was wrong? ___ ___

Add up your points and divide by 10. You will get your score per a 4.0 scale.

How Does This Text Exalt Christ?

Resting in the Shadow of the King

In Song of Songs 2:3 the bride-to-be says there is no bridegroom like her shepherd-king and that she "delights to sit in his shade and his fruit is sweet to my taste." Shulammite found rest and security in her shepherd-king because he loved her and pursued her. He sustained her and invited her to come near and experience his embrace. This shepherd-king is a wonderful picture of the One who says, "Come to Me, all of you who are weary and burdened, and I will give you rest" (Matt 11:28). In this Shepherd-King we find eternal rest and security. Here we are sustained by both "living water" (John 7:37-38) and "the bread of life" (John 6:35). We (not He!) are the lily that He has rescued from the thorns of the curse (Song 2:2; Gen 3:17-19). We are beautiful in His eyes and loved with His particular affection. We are now cleansed and made pure as His virgin bride, waiting expectantly and patiently for the consummation, "a bride adorned for her husband" (Rev 21:2). This Bridegroom also is preparing a house for us (John 14:1-3), one far more magnificent than the one Solomon built for Shulammite (Song 1:17). Shulammite saw inklings of the God of Psalm 91:1-2 where the psalmist writes, "He who dwells in the shelter of the Most High will abide in the shadow of the Almighty. I will say to the LORD, 'My refuge and my fortress, my God, in whom I trust.'"

Like the most beautiful of women, we are the object of a Shepherd-King's love. And His love can only be described as "great love" (Eph 2:4). And does He put on public display a banner that declares His love? Indeed He does! It is called the cross of Golgotha, where this King declares for the whole world to see, "I love you!"

This bride found the fruit of her king "sweet to my taste." What a blessing it is to hear that the King of kings invites us to "taste and see that the Lord is good. How happy is the one who takes refuge in Him" (Ps 34:8). His house is like no other house. His fruit is like no other fruit. His love is like no other love. Come to Jesus and eat! Come to Jesus and drink! You will find His words to be true: "No one who comes to Me will ever be hungry, and no one who believes in Me will ever be thirsty again" (John 6:35).

Reflect and Discuss

1. How does the intimacy described in these verses remind us of Eden? Why is this an important connection to make for interpretation and application?

2. Discuss the power of words in creating intimacy. How can words both help and hinder intimacy between husband and wife?

3. Have you ever failed to "say the right thing"? What did you say, and what should you have said instead?

4. Compare Solomon's home (1:16-17) with Solomon's temple (1 Kgs 5–6). What are the parallels, and what do they suggest about this text?

5. How can you affirm and celebrate the uniqueness of your spouse? What makes your spouse special?

6. Read Psalm 1. In what ways does Solomon reflect the Psalm 1 man (cf. Song 2:3-6)? How does Jesus better reflect this Psalm 1 man?

7. Discuss the biblical principles in this chapter governing sex. How do these provide helpful guidance for you in your marriage?

8. Verses 3-6 reveal great trust and affection between Solomon and Shulammite. Husbands, how can you love your wife in a manner that elicits such trust and affection? How does this love reflect Christ's love and provision for His bride?
9. Why does the broader culture marvel at and despise the idea of preserving sexual relations for marriage? Why is waiting so important that Christians should not go with the culture in this respect?
10. Read Psalm 91. In what ways does the psalmist's trust in God reflect Shulammite's trust in Solomon?

Spring Fever: Getting Ready for the Big Day

SONG OF SONGS 2:8-17

Main Idea: The love shared in marriage is filled with both dangers and delights, and at its best it points us to the love showed to us by Christ on the cross.

I. **Express Your Desire for Love (2:8-14).**
   A. Say it with your actions (2:8-9).
   B. Say it with your eyes (2:9).
   C. Say it with your words (2:10-13).
II. **Expect Some Dangers to Love (2:15).**
   A. Trouble in marriage is usually in the small things.
   B. The relationship of marriage is a uniquely sensitive thing.
III. **Enjoy the Delights of Love (2:16-17).**
   A. Know that you belong to each other (2:16).
   B. Know that you want each other (2:17).

I read a story some years ago by Norman Wright called "The 8-Cow Wife." He immediately captured my interest. Any article with such a title begs to be read! See if God doesn't teach us all something very valuable as we take it in very carefully and attentively.

> When I married my wife, we both were insecure and she did everything she could to try to please me. I didn't realize how dominating and uncaring I was toward her. My actions in our early marriage caused her to withdraw even more. I wanted her to be self-assured, to hold her head high, and her shoulders back. I wanted her to be feminine and sensual.
>
> The more I wanted her to change, the more withdrawn and insecure she felt. I was causing her to be the opposite of what I wanted her to be. I began to realize the demands I was putting on her, not so much by words but by body language.
>
> The change came about in a very interesting way. During a trip to Atlanta I read an article in *Reader's Digest*. I made a copy of it and have kept it in my heart and mind ever since.

It was the story of Johnny Lingo, a man who lived in the South Pacific. The islanders all spoke highly of this man, but when it came time for him to find a wife the people shook their heads in disbelief. In order to obtain a wife you paid for her by giving her father cows. Four to six cows was considered a high price. But the woman Johnny Lingo chose was plain, skinny and walked with her shoulders hunched and her head down. She was very hesitant and shy. What surprised everyone was Johnny's offer—he gave eight cows for her! Everyone chuckled about it, since they believed his father-in-law put one over on him.

Several months after the wedding, a visitor from the U.S. came to the islands to trade and heard the story about Johnny Lingo and his eight-cow wife. Upon meeting Johnny and his wife the visitor was totally taken back, since this wasn't a shy, plain and hesitant woman but one who was beautiful, poised and confident. The visitor asked about the transformation, and Johnny Lingo's response was very simple. "I wanted an eight-cow woman, and when I paid that for her and treated her in that fashion, she began to believe that she was an eight-cow woman. She discovered she was worth more than any other woman in the islands. And what matters most is what a woman thinks about herself." (Wright, "8-Cow Wife")

In the Song of Songs we see a similar progression with the woman we call Shulammite. From a young girl struggling with her appearance (1:6-7) and insecurities (1:7) a radiant beauty has emerged. She has grown and matured in her self-confidence and her sense of self-worth because her shepherd-king, her husband to be, has showered her with words (1:8,15-16; 2:1) and gifts (1:10-11) of affection. She knows that she is loved and it has set her free to love in return.

Our song has moved from the king's palace (1:12–2:7) back to the country and Shulammite's home (2:8-17). It is springtime and love is in the air. Their wedding day (3:6-11) and wedding night (4:1–5:1) are fast approaching. Time is growing short. Every thought, every action, and every emotion is heightened and must be carefully weighed and considered. One cannot have too much information when it comes to committing to a mate and partner for life. I believe that the most important decision a person will ever make in life is whether or not they will trust Jesus Christ as their personal Lord and Savior. I believe the second most important decision is whom they will marry. So we need to ask many good questions, look at things very carefully, and make a wise and informed decision. Sure, our hearts will be deeply involved in all of this, as well they should be! But so should our minds. What should we be looking for? What should we be communicating to the person we hope to spend the rest of our life with?

Express Your Desire for Love
SONG OF SONGS 2:8-14

In this section of the Song the bride-to-be does most of the talking. However, she spends much of her time telling us what her shepherd-king is doing and saying. This man has captured her heart, and there is so much about him she wants to share.

Five times she will call him "my love" (2:8-10,16-17). He is her king but he is also her lover. He is "*my* love." He is "my *love*." There is power and great significance in both words.

The manner in which her king expresses his love is not singular. It takes a multifaceted path that resonates with her heart and sings to her soul.

Say It with Your Actions (Song 2:8-9)

Shulammite hears Solomon before she sees him. "Listen!" she says with an air of excitement. "My love is approaching." Then suddenly she sees him and again her excitement cannot be contained. "Look! Here he comes, leaping over the mountains, bounding over the hills. My love is like a gazelle or a young stag." Today we might say, "He's a beast! He's a stud!"

His aggressiveness, agility, and attractiveness all are recognized by Shulammite. He is motivated (running, leaping) and he is interested. His actions scream loud and clear, "I want this woman!" His is a holy passion, a righteous desire, as the Song makes clear. He is enthusiastic for her. He is not ashamed to let anyone and everyone know what he feels in his heart for this lady. Her excitement for him, in return, cannot be hidden either.

Say It with Your Eyes (Song 2:9)

Suddenly he is there! "Look", she says, "he is standing behind our wall, gazing through the windows, peering through the lattice." His eyes now do some talking, and what Shulammite hears is precious indeed.

Solomon is no peeping Tom or dangerous stalker. In 5:12 she will tell him he has eyes like a dove. No, he has come to her home but he waits outside! He does not barge in rudely demanding something that does not yet belong to him. No, he approaches her with honor and respect. He comes close, very close, but not too close. His eyes tell her he loves her and that she is worth the wait. There will be a time to enter, but for now loving her with his eyes will do.

Charlotte and I once had the privilege of going to the home of Billy Graham. It was the spring of 2007. It was a wonderful visit. While we were there, he talked of his love for his wife Ruth. I will never forget what he said: "We are both old now. We can't see very well and we can't hear very well. But every morning I go to her, we hold hands, and we make love to each other with our eyes!" Wow! I pray God allows Charlotte and me to grow old like that!

Say It with Your Words (Song 2:10-13)

USA Today reported on a study that found *how* we talk, even more than what we say, can predict whether a marriage will succeed or fail:

How newlyweds talk to each other, more than what they actually say, can predict which couples will divorce with 87% accuracy, new government-sponsored research says.

The results of the 10-year study from the University of Washington, Seattle, add to the growing body of research sponsored by the National Institute of Mental Health that seeks to identify what saves marriages.

Interviewed within six months of marriage, couples who will endure already see each other "through rose-colored glasses," study co-author Sybil Carrere says. "Their behavior toward each other is positive." Those who will divorce already see each other "through fogged lenses," seeming cynical and unable to say good things about each other. (Peterson, "Sweet Nothings")

How we say things is as important as what we say. A kind attitude and a tender tone will foster receptive ears on the other end. So, for the third time Shulammite refers to Solomon as "my love." How else could she respond? With a gentleness and tenderness in his voice he speaks and she listens.

In verses 10 and 13 Solomon invites Shulammite to arise and come away with him. He is again utterly transparent in his intentions. He is also precious with his words. He calls her "my darling" and "my beautiful one." She is a joy to his heart and to his eyes. He loves her and he finds her irresistibly gorgeous. He does not keep his thoughts to himself. He does not assume she knows how he feels; he tells her how he feels. He praises her publicly and precisely.

Solomon was an atypical man when it comes to romance. He understood that the way to a woman's heart is often in the details, the little things. In verses 11-13 Solomon invites Shulammite not to have sex, but to take a walk in the countryside. She would have found this extremely romantic. Furthermore, the details with which he describes the passing of winter and the coming of spring are startling, especially for a man. It is quite likely that Solomon's elaborate description has a laser focus. Springtime is universally a time for love. Falling in love is like experiencing springtime all over again and again. Everything is fresh, new, and alive. Things simply look different when you are in love. You see things and notice things that previously you missed or overlooked. For this young couple in love, winter and the rainy days were long gone. Flowers were blooming, birds were singing, spring was in the air. You could see it and smell it (v. 13). Love could be found anywhere and everywhere you looked or turned.

When two people are in love they want to spend time alone, just the two of them. Solomon extends his invitation again, calling Shulammite his "dove" (cf. 1:15). Doves are gentle and beautiful. They often nestle in the clefts of the rock out of sight and safely hidden. Solomon compares Shulammite to such a dove and urges her to come out to him. She has kept herself safe and secure until God brought the right man into her life. She has saved herself for marriage. Now the right man has arrived and he asks her to come to him. One senses the passion of his request when he says he desires to see her lovely face and hear her sweet voice. Keel's comments strike home the thrust of Solomon's words: "the voice is just as infatuating (or 'sweet'; cf. Prov. 20:17) as the face is ravishing. . . . The usual translations ('pleasant,' 'lovely,' etc.) are too pallid, failing to do justice to the intensity that enlivens this little song" (*Song*, 107).

Craig Glickman wisely writes,

> One good indication of real love is the desire to communicate, a wish to discover all about this person whom you love so much. No detail seems too trivial to be related. No mood or feeling of one is unimportant to the other. And you care about the details and the feelings because you care so much about

the person. That which would be insignificant or boring to even a good friend is eagerly received with genuine interest by the one who loves you. . . . The mere voice of the one loved is enchantingly special just in itself. One could read from the telephone book and the other would raptly listen simply for the sound of the voice. (*Song*, 47–48)

Expect Some Dangers to Love
SONG OF SONGS 2:15

Verse 15 is one of those verses that could almost stand alone. However, the context informs us that it appears in a discussion about marriage, romance, and relationships.

Solomon uses, again, the imagery of the vineyard, but now he introduces little villains that have the potential to wreak havoc and destruction. He calls them "little foxes." They are so dangerous that he commands us to "catch" them before they "ruin the vineyards." *Catch* is an imperative. "Catch them quickly, and be aggressive about it!" is the idea.

Foxes, we are told, "were notorious in the ancient world for damaging vineyards. . . . Some ancient sources also suggest that foxes were particularly fond of grapes" (Snaith, *Song*, 41). Solomon knows the beautiful vineyard of marriage is susceptible to destructive little foxes that can sneak in without our noticing them. He also knew that "an ounce of prevention is worth a pound of cure." Better to catch them on the front end of our relationship than to have to track them down later after they have messed things up. I believe the basic thrust of Solomon's command is two-fold.

Trouble in Marriage Is Usually in the Small Things

Foxes are not large creatures. They are small and sly, sneaky and quick. They usually come out at night when you can't see them, and they are especially gifted at hiding. Often you only recognize their presence after the damage has already been done.

Two sinners saved by grace through faith in the Lord Jesus Christ are still sinners. There are details and issues we must learn to navigate and resolve. Communication, role responsibilities, finances, sex, children, in-laws, aging parents, and conflict resolution don't always (in fact, seldom!) naturally come together in a marriage relationship. What at first seems small can blow up into something big over time if it is not dealt with. Little foxes love to ruin a vineyard with bitterness, criticism, jealousy, and neglect.

In addition, ignoring them (thinking they will just go away and resolve themselves) will only encourage the foxes to mate and multiply! Recognize from the very start that the health and success of your marriage is bound up in the little things of life.

The Relationship of Marriage Is a Uniquely Sensitive Thing

The HCSB says we must be on guard against the little foxes because "our vineyards are in bloom." The NKJV says "our vines have tender grapes."

A marriage needs time to grow and bear fruit. It also needs protection because it is a tender and sensitive relationship, perhaps the most tender and sensitive of all. The fact is we all come into marriage with baggage. Open the trunk of your life and you will see both the baggage of your past and the baggage of your personality. The odds are overwhelming that you are unaware of all the things in these two bags.

Furthermore, it is almost certain that your mate has the same two bags but that the contents of those bags are altogether different from yours! Yes, it is often true that opposites attract, but it can also be true that opposites attack if we are not prepared in advance to deal with the baggage. Solomon says that little foxes can ruin the vineyards of our marriage because "our vines have tender grapes" (NKJV). They are vulnerable to attack. Therefore we must provide necessary and essential protection. In our words, actions, and attitudes we must, with dogged determination, resolve to nurture and tend to our relationship with great care and concern.

There are a number of questions that any wise couple will consider as they contemplate the prospects of marriage. These questions address various small things that could become big things if not faced head-on:

1. Have you discussed and come to agreement on what the Bible means when it says that the husband is to be a loving leader and the wife is to be gladly submissive (Eph 5:22-33)?
2. Have you agreed always to tell your spouse the truth, to speak the truth in love (Eph 4:15)?
3. Have you committed never to criticize your mate in public?
4. Are you in agreement on how decisions will be made when disagreement occurs?

5. Are you both committed to intimacy in your communication as a couple, giving the effort this will require?
6. Do you both want to be used of God to help your spouse grow in Christlikeness (Rom 8:28-30)?
7. Do you like your mate's values and outlook on life?
8. Are you personally committed to making your marriage a success whatever the cost or sacrifice?
9. Have you determined to follow biblical premarital sexual standards with honest and open discussion so that your decision honors the Lord and your partner?
10. Does the woman realize that men move from the visual to the physical (usually quickly!) and therefore they need a healthy sexual relationship with their spouses to deter temptation?
11. Does the man realize that women move from the emotional to the sexual (sometimes rather slowly) and therefore need love demonstrated in verbal and practical ways often?
12. Do you have complete confidence that your spouse will be faithful to you? I.e., can you trust her or him with a member of the opposite sex?
13. Can you identify a day or time period when you placed your faith in Jesus Christ for salvation?
14. Do you have the certainty that your mate has come to faith in the Lord Jesus Christ?
15. Has your mate demonstrated a lifestyle of similar spiritual commitments as you have?
16. Have you decided where you will attend church together (!) and to what degree you will be involved?
17. Are you comfortable sharing openly your feelings, desires, and goals with your spouse?
18. Do you experience a sense of emotional pain when you are separated from your spouse?
19. Have you demonstrated a willingness to be flexible and open to healthy compromise in your relationship?
20. Have you been able to forgive your partner for an offense, reconcile, and forget the matter (Eph 4:32)?
21. For those who are engaged, are both sets of parents in agreement with your intention to marry? If not, do they have a good reason?

22. Have you objectively looked at your fiancé's family to see the major influences shaping her or his life?
23. Do you really respect your fiancé and are you proud to have people for whom you have high regard meet him or her?
24. Do you find generally that you like the same people?
25. Have you observed differences in your social backgrounds that might cause conflicts?

Discussing and answering these questions will go a long way in handling successfully the little foxes that will attempt to wreck your relationship.

Enjoy the Delights of Love
SONG OF SONGS 2:16-17

As you consider your dating or marriage relationship, which portrays best your relationship at this time?

1. *A summer drought.* The temperature is high and your relationship is dry, suffering from a lack of vital nourishment.
2. *A fall harvest.* You are reaping some rewards in your relationship but your love is fading and cold days and nights (!) seem on the horizon.
3. *Winter deadness.* Things are frozen and lifeless.
4. *Springtime.* Life is everywhere. Things are blooming, fresh, and exciting.

It is springtime for our shepherd-king and his bride-to-be. Winter has passed. The little foxes have been captured and removed. Their vineyard, the garden, is Edenic. As a result, they are prepared to enjoy the delights of love. They know they belong to each other. They know they want each other!

Know That You Belong to Each Other (Song 2:16)

The language here is of delight and desire, confidence and assurance. "My love is mine and I am his." He belongs to me and I belong to him. There is a mutual understanding and confidence that they share. Theirs is an exclusive and intimate love. "What he wants is her and what she wants is him, exclusively and finally without remainder" (Griffiths, *Song,* 73).

The shepherd-king also "feeds among the lilies." He enjoys the delights, love, and pleasures she has to offer. He is welcome and free to browse or graze at his leisure. She gladly gives herself to this man—emotionally now, physically later—as a gift because he has given himself to her.

A biblical relationship always has two givers. There is not a giver and a taker or two takers. The husband gives himself without reserve to his wife. She, in return, is set free to give herself without reservation or hesitation. This is the beauty and glory of a redeemed, Christ-centered relationship.

Know That You Want Each Other (Song 2:17)

The couple longs for marital union and sexual consummation. Because they belong to each other they want each other with no barriers standing in the way. Thinking ahead to what they will enjoy, Shulammite invites Solomon to come into her with the agility, strength, and beauty of a gazelle or young stag (cf. 2:9). Her invitation includes an episode of all-night lovemaking. Would any red-blooded, sane male say no? "The divided mountains" could be translated "the mountains of Bether" (NIV, "the rugged hills"). Literally it is "hills or mountains of separation." This would seem to be a not-so-subtle reference to the woman's breasts (cf. 4:6). With all of his desire and passion before her, she welcomes him. "Before the day breaks [lit. "breathes"] and the shadows flee" (in other words, "all night"), be my lover and enjoy the fruits of our love. Shulammite has come a long way in her own personal self-evaluation. The unreserved love of this man who has entered her life has effected a great change. She is now the woman God created her to be. Together the two of them are far better and more beautiful than they ever could have been alone (Gen 2:18). Love will do that when we pursue it God's way and with all our heart.

Practical Applications from Song of Songs 2:8-17

50 Premarital Discussion Questions

In preparing for marriage we can never have too much information. Really knowing the person you are going to marry is essential if the marriage is going to start well, continue well, and end well. The following are some important questions prospective couples should discuss together before the "I do's." Expect some disagreement! Don't skip over and ignore the tough questions—they probably need the most attention and discussion.

1. What does love mean to you? What does it look like? Does it reflect 1 Corinthians 13?
2. Do you believe the one you love is a mature person?
3. How do you try to please the one you love?
4. Who comes first after Christ in your relationship . . . you or the one you love? Someone else?
5. How often and in what way do you express feelings of warmth, tenderness, and appreciation to the one you love?
6. What activities will you desire to continue to do separately once married?
7. How long do you want or expect your marriage to last? Why?
8. What are your strengths and weaknesses as you see yourself?
9. What do you see as your major responsibilities (or roles) in marriage?
10. What was the degree of happiness or unhappiness of your parents? What did you learn from them?
11. What feelings do you have toward each of your parents? Your brothers and sisters?
12. Did you come from a home where there were quarrels and fights? How did your parents solve differences and problems?
13. Did you favor either parent? Do you feel like you are the favorite child of either parent?
14. How did you cope with your parents when they argued?
15. How do you anticipate dealing with your parents once married? How do you anticipate dealing with your in-laws?
16. How much time do you want to spend with your parents or in-laws in the first year of marriage? After that?
17. How near do you plan to live to your parents or in-laws?
18. If a problem should come up with your parents or in-laws, who do you think should handle it?
19. Is your marriage going to be like the marriage of your parents, your in-laws, or neither? Why?
20. Is the one you love too close with either parent? Can he or she leave and cleave?
21. What form of entertainment do you like? Does the one you love enjoy the same kinds of entertainment or are they different?
22. Do you like the friends of the one you love?
23. Do you have many friends, and how close are you to them?

24. After you marry, how will you choose friends? Spend time with friends?
25. Do your feelings about God or spiritual matters play a particular, even important, part in your relationship with the one you love?
26. Do you attend church regularly? Does the one you love? Will you attend regularly and together once married?
27. Do you have a personal relationship with Jesus Christ? If not, would you like to?
28. Will any future children you may have be brought up in church and taught to love God?
29. What are your goals in life?
30. Do you like sympathy and attention when you are ill? How much do you require?
31. As a general rule, do you enjoy the companionship of the opposite sex as much as that of your own sex? How, if at all, will that change after marriage?
32. How much praise do you feel you need?
33. Do you think it will be a good idea to allow your future spouse an appropriate amount of the family income to spend as he or she chooses, without giving an account to you?
34. Do you like to tease the one you love in front of others? Why?
35. Who is more intelligent, and how do you feel about this? Who is wiser?
36. Do you ever feel depressed? Is this ever noticeable in the one you love?
37. Do you perceive yourself as a "talker" or a "listener"?
38. What interests, sports, or hobbies do you two share?
39. Do you like children? How many children do you want? How many does your future spouse want?
40. Would you express your feelings on family planning and discipline?
41. How will finances be handled in the marriage? What are your thoughts about debt?
42. Do you plan to use a budget? Have you ever tried to draw up a projected budget?
43. What sexual experience(s) have you had? Is this known to the one you love?

44. Could you express your ideas on the need for affection and sex in your forthcoming marriage?
45. Do you think your sexual needs are more or less than those of the one you love? Have you discussed this area much? At all?
46. Do you think your affectional needs are more or less than those of the one you love?
47. Who informed or instructed you on the so-called facts of life? Are you sufficiently knowledgeable in this area?
48. Do you usually remember birthdays and special occasions? How do you recognize and honor them?
49. How would you feel about getting professional help from a marriage counselor should you not be able to work out problems in your marriage?
50. Do you know many happily married couples?

How Does This Text Exalt Christ?

The Invitations of the King

In this poem the shepherd-king comes after his bride-to-be and invites her to come to him. He takes the initiative. He is the true seeker! In fact his invitations are not one, but many. And he comes to her by his voice, by his word.

In the incarnation the voice of God was heard as "the Word became flesh" (John 1:14). Coming full of grace and truth, our Shepherd-King, our Good Shepherd, informs us that like Shulammite, (1) we hear His voice, (2) He knows us, and (3) we follow [come after] Him (John 10:27). Like Shulammite we are called to "arise and come away" (Song 2:10,13) to a new life with our Shepherd-King, the Lord Jesus.

In Hebrews 3:7-19 the author cites Psalm 95:7-11, telling the people of God to "hear His voice" and enter into the rest the Lord has prepared for His people. Repeatedly He emphasized that "today" is the day to respond in faith, not hardening their hearts. Indeed their response to Him should be natural because, as Psalm 95:7 says, "He is our God and we are the people of his pasture, and the sheep of his hand."

Jesus, our Shepherd-King, invites us to come to Him now, today, for rest in a garden of love, joy, and fruitfulness made possible by way of another garden, the garden of Gethsemane. Coming to Him in faith, we can proclaim for all to hear, "My beloved is mine and I am his" (2:16). His voice, His word, is the only voice I want to hear. His voice, His word, is all I need to hear. Today, as I hear His voice, I will not harden my heart. Rather, I will let His voice put me at ease and bring joy to my soul, for my beloved Lord Jesus is mine and I am His!

Reflect and Discuss

1. What are some ways to communicate your love for your spouse with your actions? Why is it important to use various means to communicate love?
2. Discuss with your spouse how you use words to communicate affection to one another. Are you clear and encouraging? Are you specific in expressing your love?
3. What are some "foxes" that are likely to attack almost any marriage? What are some that you have seen in your own relationships?
4. Why is it important to remember that all marriages are made up of two sinful people? How should we expect this to affect our marriages?
5. What are some practical ways to protect your marriage morally? Spiritually? Emotionally?
6. Discuss the list of "small things that could become big things." Where is your marriage most at risk? Where is it most protected against attack?
7. Why must a biblical relationship consist of two givers? What are some things each person should seek to give to the other?
8. Read through and discuss the questions for those preparing for marriage. Where are there significant agreements and disagreements between you and your (future) mate?
9. In what ways does getting married parallel our salvation experience? What passages would you use to draw the parallels?
10. Solomon pursued Shulammite because he set his love on her. Reflect on how Christ likewise set His love on you and pursued you, a sinner in need of grace.

Men Are from Earth and Women Are from Earth (Part 1)

So Deal with the Dangerous Foxes

SONG OF SONGS 2:15

Main Idea: Every marriage will face many trials from without and within, but God in Christ empowers believers to guard against sin and pursue a God-honoring picture of His grace.

I.   Beware of the Fox of Role Reversal or Abuse.
II. Beware of the Fox of Intimacy Stagnation.
III. Beware of the Fox of Poor Communication.
IV. Beware of the Fox of Time Ill Spent.
V.   Beware of the Fox of Outside Interference.
VI. Beware of the Fox of Fatigue.
VII. Beware of the Fox of Misunderstanding.

John Gray became a household name and an overnight millionaire in the 1990s with his blockbuster *Men Are from Mars, Women Are from Venus.* The book has sold more than 50 million copies, has been translated into at least 50 different languages, and spent 121 weeks on the bestseller list. Published in 1992, CNN said it was the highest ranked work of non-fiction of the 1990s (CNN, "Grisham Ranks").

His book did well because it struck a chord that we all see and understand: men and women are different. Indeed we are different by design! Genesis 1:27 is crystal clear: "So God created man in His own image; He created him in the image of God; He created them male and female." And Moses adds in Genesis 1:31, "God saw all that He had made, and it was very good."

However, John Gray is not precisely correct in his analysis. Men are not from Mars and women are not from Venus. Men are from Earth and women are from Earth, and we must learn to deal with it. Further, because of the invasion of sin into God's good creation (Gen 3), things no longer work as our Lord intended. Sin and its dangers are always lurking about, dangers Solomon calls "little foxes that ruin the vineyard."

The word *catch* in verse 15 is an imperative, a word of command. God issues a strong word about this danger to our relationship. The little foxes are unwelcome intruders that sneak into a marriage and can destroy the purity of our love and the pricelessness of our relationship. A healthy and happy marriage must be protected. We must be on guard and catch anything that could harm the tender and vulnerable union we have established. Now a question naturally presents itself: What do these little foxes look like? Let me highlight seven of the more common species that have harmed and destroyed far too many marriages.

Beware of the Fox of Role Reversal or Abuse

The Bible teaches that God created us male and female (Gen 1:27). It teaches that the Lord made a woman as a man's helper and complement (Gen 2:18,20-24). Further, the New Testament instructs us that a woman is to submit to her husband gladly and that a husband is to love his wife sacrificially (Eph 5:22-33; Col 3:18-19; 1 Pet 3:1-7). This is the divinely ordained structure God has established for marriage. However, if these roles get reversed or abused, a marriage will get into trouble. So let's strive for clarity on this issue.

God made men to be men, husbands, and fathers. A man should never apologize for being a man, for being a masculine human being. God made women to be women, wives, and mothers. No woman should ever apologize for being the feminine person our Lord designed her to be. You see, no one is as good at being a man as a man, and no one is as good at being a woman as a woman. However, there is great confusion about gender roles today. Men, in particular, are suffering an identity crisis. In our day, men struggle with their maleness. Being the provider and protector (1 Tim 5:8) is challenged and even rejected by an increasingly feminized and gender-confused culture. Let me provide just one example. In a book review for the book *Manliness* by Harvey C. Mansfield, a woman named Christina Sommers notes,

> One of the least visited memorials in Washington is a
> waterfront statue commemorating the men who died on
> the *Titanic*. Seventy-four percent of the women passengers

survived the April 15, 1912, calamity, while 80 percent of the men perished. Why? Because the men followed the principle "women and children first."

The monument, an 18-foot granite male figure with arms outstretched to the side, was erected by "the women of America" in 1931 to show their gratitude. The inscription reads: "To the brave men who perished in the wreck of the Titanic. . . . They gave their lives that women and children might be saved."

Today, almost no one remembers those men. Women no longer bring flowers to the statue on April 15 to honor their chivalry. The idea of male gallantry makes many women nervous, suggesting (as it does) that women require special protection. It implies the sexes are objectively different. It tells us that some things are best left to men. Gallantry is a virtue that dare not speak its name.

In *Manliness*, Harvey C. Mansfield seeks to persuade skeptical readers, especially educated women, to reconsider the merits of male protectiveness and assertiveness. It is in no way a defense of male privilege, but many will be offended by its old-fashioned claim that the virtues of men and women are different and complementary. Women would be foolish not to pay close attention to Mansfield's subtle and fascinating argument. (Sommers, "Being a Man")

Men and women must stand strong in the truths of Scripture concerning our identity and assignments. We must not be swept along by the floodtides of modernity that try to redefine and even destroy the image of God that men and women uniquely bear as gender-distinctive individuals. God's creation of us as male and female is good. He did not make a mistake.

Beware of the Fox of Intimacy Stagnation

Proverbs 30:18-19 says, "Three things are beyond me; four I can't understand: the way of an eagle in the sky, the way of a snake on a rock, the way of a ship at sea, and *the way of a man with a young woman*" (emphasis added). The progress of love is marvelous and mysterious. There is something exceptional and special when a young couple falls in love. That initial sensual attraction is strong. It is almost irresistible. It is one of the reasons we marry! The apostle Paul reminds us when it comes to passion for intimacy, "It is better to marry than to burn with desire" (1 Cor 7:9).

Now this youthful passion and sensual desire may be enough to get us started, but it is not enough to get us to the finish line together. What we start with must grow wider and deeper if we are to enjoy and experience all that our God desires. That which begins physical and sensual must also be spiritual and personal.

I am convinced that the key to capturing the little fox of intimacy stagnation is growing to become one another's best friends. In this Song, that is exactly what we see happening. Solomon calls his wife "my darling," but he will also call her "my sister" (4:12; 5:2). Shulammite will call her husband "my love" (repeatedly!), but she will also refer to him as "my friend" (5:16). Living and sharing life together over the years of a long and lasting marriage opens the door to an intimacy you have no idea even exists when you first get started. There is no way you can know, except by growing in your knowledge, love, and understanding of one another. And this takes time.

When Charlotte and I married I was 21 and she was 19. I want you to know that I loved her. But today, several decades later, I want the whole world to know that I really, really love her. I had no idea a love, friendship, and intimacy like this was possible when we first began. And I have no doubt it is one of the blessings of marriage the Lord desires for every marriage.

Beware of the Fox of Poor Communication

Proverbs 15:1-2 reminds us, "A gentle answer turns away anger, but a harsh word stirs up wrath. The tongue of the wise makes knowledge attractive, but the mouth of fools blurts out foolishness." And for good measure, Proverbs 15:4 adds, "The tongue that heals is a tree of life, but a devious [NIV, "perverse"] tongue breaks the spirit."

We now know that for a marriage to be healthy and vibrant, five areas require consistent monitoring and attention: (1) communication, (2) finances, (3) sex, (4) children, and (5) in-law relationships. Aging parents is a sixth item on this list for many. If any of the last four or five issues become problematic, you can be sure that communication broke down. To walk together for a lifetime requires that we talk and listen well on a regular basis.

In his book *Why Marriages Succeed or Fail,* marriage and family researcher John Gottman identifies what he calls "The Four Horsemen of the Apocalypse That Can Destroy Your Marriage." Interestingly, all four are related to communication:

Criticism: When you criticize your spouse you are basically implying that there is something wrong with him or her. Using the words "You always" and "You never" are common ways to criticize. When you use these phrases, your spouse is most likely to feel under attack and to respond defensively. This is a dangerous pattern because neither person feels heard and both may begin to feel bad about themselves or inadequate in the presence of the other. The antidote to criticism is to make a direct and specific complaint that is not a global attack on your spouse's person.

Defensiveness: When you attempt to defend yourself from a perceived attack with a counter complaint, you are being defensive. Another way people are defensive is to whine like an innocent victim. Unfortunately, defensiveness keeps partners from taking responsibility for problems and it usually escalates negative communication. Even if your mate is criticizing you, defensiveness is not an appropriate response. It will only fuel a bad exchange. The antidote to defensiveness is to try to hear your partner's complaint and to take some responsibility for the problem.

Contempt: Contempt is any statement or nonverbal behavior that puts you on a higher ground than your spouse. Mocking your spouse, calling him or her names, rolling your eyes, and sneering in disgust are all examples of contempt. Of all the horsemen, contempt is the most dangerous and serious. Couples have to realize that these types of put-downs will destroy the fondness and admiration they share. The antidote to contempt is to lower your tolerance for contemptuous statements and behaviors and to actively work on building a culture of appreciation in the relationship. Is it easy? No. Can it be done? Yes.

Stonewalling: Stonewalling happens when the listener withdraws from the conversation. The stonewaller might actually physically leave or they may just stop tracking with the conversation and appear to shut down. The stonewaller may look like he doesn't care (80% are men), but that usually isn't the case. Typically they are overwhelmed and are trying to calm themselves. Unfortunately, this seldom works because the mate, especially if it is the woman, is likely to assume they don't care enough about the problem to talk about it. It can be a vicious circle with one person demanding to talk and the other looking for an escape. The antidote is to learn to identify the signs that you or your spouse is starting to feel emotionally overwhelmed and to agree together to take a break. If the problem still needs to be discussed then pick it up when you are calmer and more rested.

Good communication is hard work. It is also worthwhile work. It is not something that comes easy. It requires us to express ourselves clearly and lovingly (Eph 4:15). It also requires that we listen attentively and eagerly (Jas 1:19). It requires us to "be doers of the word and not hearers only, deceiving ourselves" (Jas 1:22). It demands that "No foul language is to come from [our] mouth, but only what is good for building up someone in need, so that it gives grace to those who hear" (Eph 4:29).

Beware of the Fox of Time Ill Spent

Ephesians 5:15-16 says, "Pay careful attention, then, to how you walk—not as unwise people but as wise—making the most of the time, because the days are evil." A marriage will get into trouble when forces or persons outside the marriage encroach on the all-important time the two people need alone to build and maintain a healthy relationship. *Love* is a beautiful four-letter word. Sometimes it is best spelled T-I-M-E. A marriage is headed for hard times if our best time is given to things that promise only a small return on our investment.

I'm not a hunter, but I have many friends who delight in such foolishness (I mean, recreational activities!). To be honest, I don't think their elevator reaches the penthouse, if you know what I mean. Now let's think about it for a minute. Here is a guy with two options. Option 1: He can, at 4:00 a.m., climb up into a tree in a contraption called a deer stand and freeze while waiting to shoot Bambi. Option 2: He can be back home in a nice warm bed holding his woman. This is a no-brainer as far as I can tell! Now let me be fair. I'm not against hunting, fishing, or many other good things like this that men and women do. What I am against is giving our best time and quantity time to things that really do not matter, that are not the most important. And there are a couple of new and extremely dangerous foxes in the woods who are doing some serious damage in this area. One is called "the Internet." The other is called "video games."

The Internet, with access to pornography on the one hand and cyber romances on the other, has become a major breeding ground for adultery and infidelity. It has also become an enslaving and cruel taskmaster for many males who do not grow into the men that God created them to be. Interestingly, the average male video game player is now 35![3]

All of us must take control of our calendars and spend our time well and wisely. We must avoid the places of temptation. And we must learn the art of saying "no" to even good things so that we might say "yes" to the better and best things. James 4:14 says our life is "a mist that appears for a little while and then vanishes." We do not want to get to the end of that mist and look back with regret for the time ill spent.

Beware of the Fox of Outside Interference

The Bible warns us about the deadly and destructive power of adultery. Listen to the warning and wisdom of Proverbs 5:1-14:

> My son, pay attention to my wisdom;
> listen closely to my understanding
> so that you may maintain discretion
> and your lips safeguard knowledge.
> Though the lips of the forbidden woman drip honey
> and her words are smoother than oil,
> in the end she's as bitter as wormwood
> and as sharp as a double-edged sword.
> Her feet go down to death;
> her steps head straight for Sheol.
> She doesn't consider the path of life;
> she doesn't know that her ways are unstable.
> So now, my son, listen to me,
> and don't turn away from the words of my mouth.
> Keep your way far from her.
> Don't go near the door of her house.
> Otherwise, you will give up your vitality to others
> and your years to someone cruel;
> strangers will drain your resources,
> and your earnings will end up in a foreigner's house.

---

[3] *American Journal of Preventive Medicine* 37, no. 4 (October 2009): 299–305.

At the end of your life, you will lament
when your physical body has been consumed,
and you will say, "How I hated discipline,
and how my heart despised correction.
I didn't obey my teachers
or listen closely to my mentors.
I am on the verge of complete ruin
before the entire community."

What are the warning signs this dangerous and evil fox may be lurking near, hiding out in, your vineyard? Carefully consider these 10:

1. Feelings of "going through the marriage motions."
2. Inventing excuses to visit someone of the opposite sex.
3. Increasing male-female contacts in normal environments (e.g., work, sharing meals, recreation).
4. Being preoccupied with thoughts about another person.
5. Exchanging gifts with a "friend" of the opposite sex.
6. Making daily or weekly contact with someone by phone.
7. Putting yourself in situations where a "friend" or "employee" might become something more.
8. Having to touch, embrace, or glance at a person of the opposite sex.
9. Spending time alone with anyone of the opposite sex.
10. Inordinate time on the Internet.

These are just a few of the foxes that open the door to an affair, to adultery. It comes about slowly, over time, almost without notice. It is a deadly and devastating fox that will take you where you don't want to go and cost you so much more than you want to pay. Paul says in 1 Corinthians 6:18, "Run from sexual immorality." Wiser words have never been written.

Beware of the Fox of Fatigue

Marriages get in trouble when the wedding vows are considered conditional. They get in trouble when marriage is no longer considered a sacred covenant before God. They get in trouble when divorce begins to be considered as a possible solution to an unhappy situation.

Let me be both a prophet and a pastor at this point. First, the prophet: God hates divorce, and He is not ambivalent about it. In Malachi 2:16 the Bible says, "'For I hate divorce,' says the LORD" (NASB). And in Matthew 19:6 Jesus says, "Therefore, what God has joined together, man must not separate." God designed marriage to be permanent. He planned for it to last "until death do us part." We must not surrender this ideal. We must not lower the standard.

However, and now I will be the pastor, we live in a fallen and broken world where sinful things happen, including divorce. Rocks should never be thrown at those who have suffered the pain and sorrow of divorce. Instead, we extend marvelous grace and redeeming love. We claim the promise of 1 John 1:9 that "if we confess our sins, He is faithful and righteous to forgive us our sins and to cleanse us from all unrighteousness." We acknowledge that we cannot change our past, but by God's grace, for His glory, and for our good, we can do something about our present and our future. Daily we should recommit ourselves to a lasting and lifelong marriage that reflects the beautiful covenant relationship of Christ and His church (Eph 5:21-33). Divorce simply will not be an option. We will, with God's help, find our way through any and every problem because we are in this thing called marriage together and to the end. We are as committed to one another as our God is committed to us, as Christ is committed to His church.

Beware of the Fox of Misunderstanding

We have repeatedly emphasized that God made men and women different and that He did so by divine design (Gen 1–2). I think it is sometimes helpful to consider this truth playfully. After all, being serious all the time is not conducive to good marital health!

I have often said that men are like dogs and women are like cats. I have good evidence for this conviction. Think about it. A man is like a dog: If you feed him, praise him, and play with him on a regular basis, you will have a happy man. On the other hand a woman is far more complex and mysterious, much like a cat: A cat can walk into a room; you look at it, and it looks at you. It walks over to you and begins to purr and rub up against your leg in a sweet and gentle fashion. The cat then quickly turns around and walks out of the room, and you say, "That was a really sweet cat." However, a few minutes later that same cat walks into the room; you look at it, and it looks at you. Suddenly without provocation or warning, the cat leaps for your face and tries to claw out your eyeballs! Now that was the same cat that came in so sweet and gentle a few moments ago. But something happened while that cat was out of the room. You have no idea what it was, but it certainly changed the disposition of that cat in a matter of seconds. There are some significant similarities between a cat and a woman!

A friend of mine heard me draw this analogy some years ago, and he sent me something that reinforced my thesis that men are dogs and women are cats. I suspect you will enjoy this!

Is It a Cat? Is It a Woman? Maybe It's Both! Why?

- They do what they want.
- They rarely listen to you.
- They're totally unpredictable.
- They wail when they are not happy.
- When you want to play, they want to be alone.
- When you want to be alone, they want to play.
- They expect you to cater to their every whim.
- They're moody.
- They can drive you nuts and cost you an arm and a leg.
- They leave their hair everywhere.

Is It a Dog? Is It a Man? Maybe It's Both! Why?

- They lie around all day, sprawled out on the most comfortable piece of furniture in the house.
- They can hear a package of food opening half a block away, but they can't hear you even when you're in the same room.
- They leave their toys everywhere.
- They growl when they are not happy.
- When you want to play, they want to play.
- When you want to be left alone, they still want to play.
- They are great at begging.
- They will love you forever if you feed them and rub their tummies.
- They do disgusting things with their mouths and then try to give you a kiss.
- They can look dumb and lovable all at the same time.

Yes, men and women really are different, and they are different in some significant ways. You would almost think someone designed it that way!

Practical Applications from Song of Songs 2:15

A number of years ago Harry Chapin wrote a song entitled, "We Grew Up a Little Bit." He did not have many answers, but he sure knew how to raise the right questions. The words of this song are powerful. They challenge your heart and your commitment to each other to grow at least a little bit every single day in this precious relationship we call marriage.

The song tells of two young people who get married, which makes them grow up a little bit. The struggles of getting started and working menial jobs make them grow a little more, but also lead to conflict—which also makes them grow a little. As they spiral down into a dead marriage, and as abuse enters the picture, the singer questions whether they really have been growing at all. The song ends with the question of whether they could start over and start growing from this point forward.

How Does This Text Exalt Christ?

My Shepherd-King Has Dealt With the Little Foxes

The gospel of Jesus Christ transforms us into "a new creation" (2 Cor 5:17). We see things with new eyes. Our hearts are transformed with new affections.

Let's make specific application to men in this study. A husband is now able to live with his wife with "understanding of their weaker nature yet showing them honor as coheirs of the grace of life" (1 Pet 3:7). To use the imagery of our Song, a husband becomes more sensitive to "the little foxes that ruin the vineyards." He, as a gospel-transformed man, is no longer corrupted by deceitful desires. Rather, he is daily renewed in the spirit of his mind in righteousness and purity of the truth. He doesn't speak lies to his wife, but tells her the truth. He will not go to bed angry with her, but will take whatever time and energy necessary to work through their conflicts and disagreements. With a Christ-confidence and conviction, he determines not to give the Devil an opportunity (Eph 4:22-27). "None of these little foxes will invade my vineyard!" he says.

Further, he spots the little foxes that love to corrupt our conversations. With the aid of the Holy Spirit, he strives mightily to kick from the vineyard the foxes of bitterness, anger, wrath, shouting, slander, and malice. Finally, after dispensing with these little foxes, he replaces them with the blossoms, flowers, and fragrances of kindness, compassion, and forgiveness. Indeed, he chooses, as an act of his will, to forgive his wife of any and all offenses "just as God also forgave [him] in Christ" (Eph 4:30-32). You see, the little foxes that can harm our marriage have been dealt with at Calvary. They have been nailed to the cross. Christ has already put to death the little foxes that ruin the vineyard. The victory for our marriages is already accomplished. It is ours for the taking!

Reflect and Discuss

1. What are some ways you see our culture confused about the differences between men and women? What are some biblical passages that shed light on those differences?
2. What might role reversal look like in a marriage? What might it look like for men or women to abuse their roles?
3. Why is the passion of early romance insufficient to carry a marriage through a lifetime? How can couples cultivate deeper intimacy throughout their marriage?
4. How have you seen failure to communicate manifest as a fox in your relationships? Do you default to any of the "four horsemen"?
5. What are some of the less important things in your life that could become dangerous foxes by consuming too much of your time?
6. What practical steps can you take to obey Paul's instruction in 1 Corinthians 6:18 to "run from sexual immorality"?
7. How can the differences between men and women lead to misunderstanding? How can these misunderstandings lead to troubles in a marriage relationship?
8. Discuss how Christ's finished work impacts our continued work of ridding our homes of foxes.

9. Discuss the role of the Holy Spirit in recognizing and fighting against foxes.
10. What are some other foxes you see warned against in the Scriptures? How can we be on guard against these?

Men Are from Earth and Women Are from Earth (Part 2)

So Deal with the Different Foxes

SONG OF SONGS 2:15

Main Idea: Though the differences between men and women pose serious challenges to a marriage in a broken world, the power of the gospel enables and empowers believers to cultivate "beautiful vineyards" that reflect God's character.

I. Men and Women Communicate Differently.
II. Men and Women See Romance Differently.
III. Men and Women Are Wired Differently.
IV. Men and Women See Self-Worth Differently.
V. Men and Women View Time Differently.
VI. Men and Women Parent Differently.

I believe that God wants us to make much of Jesus Christ in our marriage and family. I believe He wants us to show a confused and hurting world the greatness of Christ in the most challenging and intimate of all relationships. I believe our God wants to show those enslaved to sin that Jesus Christ makes a difference, a real difference, today and forever.

A Christ-centered, God-focused marriage will aggressively be on guard against what Solomon calls the "little foxes." He commands us to be on the lookout for these marital varmints that can, by stealth, sneak into our home and inflict major damage.

Unlike so much popular culture in the western world, the Bible does not pit man against woman in a "battle of the sexes." God's intention from the beginning is that the two would "become one flesh" (Gen 2:24). God's design is one of harmonious union, with each one loving and serving the other in a complementary relationship. The little foxes are determined to see that this does not happen. Fueled by the evil one and our fallen, sinful, and selfish desires, they will, in particular, attack our God-given differences and turn them into differences that damage and destroy. Therefore, it is good for us to look more closely at some of the ways that God made men and women different. Being aware of and sensitive to these realities is good preventative medicine that will go a long way in fighting off the little foxes that attempt to infest the beautiful vineyard God has given us.

Men and Women Communicate Differently

Good communication is important in building healthy relationships in life. It is absolutely essential in building a healthy relationship in marriage. James warns us that a tongue out of control "is a fire . . . a world of unrighteousness. . . . It pollutes the whole body . . . and is set on fire by hell" (Jas 3:6). The apostle Paul challenges us, "Your speech should always be gracious, seasoned with salt, so that you may know how you should answer each person" (Col 4:6).

Communicating well can be a real challenge in marriage because men and women do this thing differently. Men are often intimidated when it comes to communication because we are not nearly as good at it as women are. Listening well for an extended period of time is hard work for a man. However, it nurtures intimacy and brings happiness to a woman. She finds it nourishing to her heart and soul.

Men tend to be fact-based: "Just the facts please!" Women, in stark contrast, want to share their feelings. They also like to provide a big context, bringing in lots of details that can seem unnecessary to a man.

Men feel compelled to offer solutions when asked a question, but often a woman simply wants affirmation and reassurance that you are listening and that you care. Unfortunately, men are not good at picking up on hints. Women, however, are often subtle and coded in their conversation. The tone of her voice, the look in her eyes, or her body language may be speaking the message her husband should be listening for.

Yes, communication is a challenging assignment for a husband and wife, but working hard at it brings massive blessings and rewards. It is worth the effort, for as Proverbs 16:24 says, "Pleasant words are a honeycomb: sweet to the taste and health to the body."

Men and Women See Romance Differently

Genesis 2:25 tells us that in the garden of Eden, before the fall, "Both the man and his wife were naked, yet felt no shame." Later the author of Hebrews would add, "Marriage is honorable among all, and the bed undefiled" (Heb 13:4 NKJV). So sex is clearly a good gift from a great God to be enjoyed within covenantal marriage between a man and a woman. However—and this is something many men don't get—the context for sex is romance. It is an environment of romance that fosters an active and meaningful sex life. Herein lies a significant challenge.

Romance for a man is often a three-letter word: S-E-X. Indeed, to consider romance apart from sex is virtually impossible for almost any red-blooded male. In contrast, romance for a woman can mean lots of things, and sex may or may not be included! The fact is—and this is so important—women find some of the most interesting (and to men, surprising) things romantic: praying with her, helping her with the dishes, cleaning out the garage, or running a warm bubble bath and lighting a candle. All of these things are strange to a male, but they speak deeply to the heart of a woman.

The simple fact is men and women are wired differently when it comes to the area of romance. For men, romance is highly visual; it is what they see. For women, romance is extremely relational and personal; it is what they feel. Men indeed are creatures of sight; they are moved by what they see. Women on the other hand are creatures of the ear and the heart; they are moved by what they hear and by what they feel.

This point is so crucial it might be worth our digressing for just a moment. What do men say romance is to them? The following list of 15 suggestions from Gary Chapman's excellent book *Toward a Growing Marriage* is not exhaustive, but it is helpful as a woman tries to understand where a man is coming from in this area of romance.

1. Be attractive at bedtime—nothing in the hair or strange on the face. Wear something besides granny gowns and pajamas.
2. Do not be ashamed to show you enjoy being with me.
3. Dress more appealingly when I am at home (no housecoats, slippers, etc.).
4. Do things to catch my attention: remember that a man is easily excited by *sight.*
5. Communicate more openly about sex.
6. Do not make me feel guilty at night for my inconsistencies during the day (such as not being affectionate enough).
7. Be more aware of my needs and desires as a man.

8. Show more desire, and understand that caressing and foreplay are as important to me as they are to you.
9. Do not allow yourself to remain upset over everyday events that go wrong.
10. Do not try to fake enjoyment. Be authentic in your response to me.
11. Do not try to punish me by denying me sex or by giving it grudgingly.
12. Treat me like your lover.
13. Listen to my suggestions on what you can do to improve our sexual relationship.
14. Forgive me when I fall short of what I should be.
15. Tell me what I can do to be the sexual partner you desire. (Chapman, *Toward a Growing Marriage*, 161–62)

On the other hand, what suggestions have wives made to their husbands as to how they can make romance and sexual relations more meaningful? Again, this list is to help us get the idea.

1. Show more affection; give me attention throughout the day; come in after work and kiss me on my neck and ask me about my day (and stay around to listen!).
2. Be more sympathetic when I am really sick.
3. Accept me as I am; accept me even when you see the worst side of me.
4. Tell me that you love me at times other than when we are in bed; phone sometimes just to say, "I love you!" Do not be ashamed to tell me "I love you" in front of others.
5. While I am bathing or showering, find soft music on the radio or dim the lights and light a candle.
6. Honor Christ as the head of our home.
7. Talk to me after our lovemaking; make caresses after our lovemaking and hold me.
8. Be sweet and loving (at least one hour) before initiating sex.
9. Show an interest in what I have to say in the morning.
10. Help me wash dinner dishes and clean the kitchen.
11. Pay romantic attention to me (hold hands, kiss) even during relatively unromantic activities (television watching, car riding, walking in the mall, etc.).

12. Help me feel that I am sexually and romantically attractive by complimenting me more often.
13. Pray with me about the problems and victories you are having; let me express my own needs to you.
14. Do not approach lovemaking as a ritualistic activity, make each time a new experience.
15. Think of something nice to say about me and do it in front of others often (Chapman, *Toward a Growing Marriage*, 162–64).

Men and Women Are Wired Differently

Genesis 1:27 teaches us that God created us "male and female." From the inside out our Creator hardwired us differently—emotionally, psychologically, and physically. These innate differences can be observed in a number of interesting ways. For example, a woman wants to feel valued by her man, that she is important to him. She wants to be nourished and cherished by him (Eph 5:29). A man, on the other hand, needs to feel successful. He is motivated to achieve the goals he has set for himself. He fears few things more than failure, especially in providing for his family. This should not surprise us. First Timothy 5:8 says if a man "does not provide for his own, that is his own household, he has denied the faith and is worse than an unbeliever."

A woman also loves to be listened to, especially at the heart level. In contrast, a man, like his canine companion, responds to praise. It addresses his God-given need for respect and admiration (Eph 5:33). Some years ago I came across a short article in the monthly *Focus on the Family* magazine derived from the book *Now We're Talking* by Robert and Pamela Crosby that playfully (and insightfully!) highlighted the point I am trying to make. It addresses both what is really important to a man and woman, as well as what they really mean by what they say. Now there are always exceptions to what follows, but there is a world of truth here as well!

Remember What's Important to a Woman

- Make sure you have *time* to listen. She can tell when you are really interested and when you are merely humoring her.
- A woman needs to know that a man is *genuinely listening*—listening with his heart and not trying to figure out how to "fix" her problem.
- She needs to feel free to share her opinion and to help her husband understand without him getting frustrated or angry.

- A woman needs to feel valued by her husband beyond all of his human relationships.
- A woman values relational moments far more than occupational achievements.
- A woman is deeply affirmed when a man makes a noticeable effort to hear her heart.

Remember What's Important to a Man

- When men become uncaring or distant toward you, it is usually because they are afraid of something.
- Men tend to "report" more than converse. Just listen to a man on the phone. Usually, his comments are brief, utilitarian, and to the point. "Okay . . . got it . . . be there at 8 . . . see ya soon."
- Men are more motivated to achieve goals than to absorb moments.
- Men fear nothing more than failure.
- Men are motivated by feeling significant.
- Men want to manage their own problems and be "Mr. Fix-It"!
- Men want to "get to the bottom line."

What a Woman Says and What She Means

When she says	She really means
"We need."	"I want."
"Do what you want."	"You'll pay for this later!"
"Sure . . . go ahead."	"I don't want you to do that!"
"The kitchen is so inconvenient."	"I want a new house."
"The trash is full."	"Take it out!"
"Nothing is wrong."	"Everything is wrong."
"I don't want to talk about it."	"Go away. I'm still building up steam."
"Am I fat?"	"Tell me I'm beautiful."
"You have to learn to communicate."	"Just agree with me."
"Are you listening?"	"Too late. You're dead."

What a Man Says and What He Means

When he says	He really means
"Boy, am I hungry!"	"Make me something and serve it to me on the couch."
"It's too expensive."	"You could get a neat computer for that!"
"It's a beautiful day."	"It's too hot for yard work!"
"I have a surprise."	"I bought something stupid."
"Why don't you get a job?"	"You bought something really stupid."
"You can't mow the lawn when the grass is wet."	"There's a game on the tube." (Adapted from Crosby and Crosby, *Now We're Talking*)

Men and Women See Self-Worth Differently

In a world drowning in the idolatries of the self, radical autonomy, and self-esteem, we need a healthy dose of biblical realism and balance. Men and women equally bear the image of God. Men and women are also equally depraved and sinful, in desperate need of radical grace. In Christ we obtain a "self-worth" that is a bona fide reality we should affirm and rejoice in (2 Cor 5:17). There is a theologically authentic sense in which I should see my value and worth both by creation and by redemption. This will breed both humility and a genuine sense of significance because this is how I am seen by my Creator and Redeemer.

Now, how men and women understand their self-worth, how they experience self-worth in the living of life, is usually quite different. Women tend to be far more relational. My friend Barbara O'Chester says women "love to make a memory" and that they do so primarily in relationships, especially with their family and friends. Men gauge their value in the things they do, such as how they make a living.

To ground this again in biblical revelation, a husband should cultivate his sense of self-worth as he loves his wife well (Eph 5:25-33) and grows in his understanding of her (1 Pet 3:7). This draws the smile of God and is a cause for rejoicing. A wife can see her value and self-worth as she graciously submits to her husband and honors him with her respect (Eph 5:22-24,33). The pattern for church life laid out so beautifully in Titus 2:1-8 provides assignments for men and women that involve not only our faith community, but also the family. Identity in

Christ and activity for His glory are the right avenues for how we see ourselves. In our Savior we can truly say, "I am somebody!"

Men and Women View Time Differently

Psalm 90:12 says, "Teach us to number our days carefully so that we may develop wisdom in our hearts." This is great wisdom for a husband/father and a wife/mother. A man, in particular, needs to heed this sage advice. You see, men do not think much about time. Women, however, value both quantity and quality time. Baby boomers, my generation, bought into a great lie. We told ourselves that though we did not give our children quantity time because of the busyness of our schedules, we more than made up for it with quality time. However, we now know that for a child, and for that matter a spouse, quality time *is* quantity time. Both a spouse and children want you when they want you, and if you're not there, they don't get you. Men too often simply go with the flow. Before they realize it the sand in the hourglass has almost run out. Looking back over the years now gone, their hearts are filled with regret for the time now lost with their mate and children, with no possibility of getting it back.

Reba McEntire, a country singer, recorded a song many years ago written by Richard Leigh and Layng Martine Jr. It could tragically be the theme song of many a daughter or son as they reflect on this issue of time as it relates to their daddy.

"The Greatest Man I Never Knew"

The greatest man I never knew
Lived just down the hall.
And every day we said hello
But never touched at all.
He was in his paper.
I was in my room.
How was I to know, he thought I hung the moon?

The greatest man I never knew
Came home late every night.
He never had too much to say,
Too much was on his mind.
I never really knew him,

And now it seems so sad.
Everything he gave to us took all he had.

Then the days turned into years,
And the memories to black and white.
He grew cold like an old winter wind
Blowing across my life.

The greatest words I never heard
I guess I'll never hear.
The man I thought could never die
Been dead almost a year.
He was good at business,
But there was business left to do.
He never said he loved me, guess he thought I knew.[4]

Men and Women Parent Differently

God designed children with a need both for a dad and a mom (Eph 6:1-4;
Col 3:20-21). They need both because their parents bring different abili-
ties and gifts into the dynamics of family life. God designed mothers to
nurture and provide the emotional support that is necessary for the
healthy development of a child. Fathers provide strength and a child's
sense of self-worth and security. Amazingly, even the simple presence
of the man in the home can make a tremendous impact on the life of
a child. That's why the death of a father is so hurtful. But the loss of
a father by divorce is utterly tragic. One of my favorite theologians is
Erma Bombeck. In her book *Family—the Ties That Bind . . . and Gag!* she
illustrates beautifully the importance that the presence of a father can
make in the life of a child:

> One morning my father didn't get up and go to work. He went
> to the hospital and died the next day.
>
>   I hadn't thought that much about him before. He was just
> someone who left and came home and seemed glad to see
> everyone at night. He opened the jar of pickles when no one

---

[4] "The Greatest Man I Ever Knew," written by Richard C. Leigh and Laying Martine ©
1991 EMI April Music Inc. & Lion-Hearted Music & Publisher(s) Unknown. All rights on
behalf of EMI April Music Inc. & Lion-Hearted Music administered by Sony/ATV Music
Publishing LLC., 424 Church Street, Nashville, TN 37219. All rights reserved. Used by
permission.

else could. He was the only one in the house who wasn't afraid
to go into the basement by himself.

He cut himself shaving, but no one kissed it or got excited
about it. It was understood when it rained, he got the car and
brought it around to the door. When anyone was sick, he went
to get the prescription filled. He took lots of pictures . . . but
he was never in them.

Whenever I played house, the Mother doll had a lot to do.
I never knew what to do with the Daddy doll, I had him say,
"I'm going off to work now" and threw him under the bed.

The funeral was in our living room and a lot of people
came and brought all kinds of good food and cakes. We had
never had so much company before.

[Later,] I went to my room and felt under the bed for the
Daddy doll. When I found him, I dusted him off and put him
on my bed.

He never did anything. I didn't know his leaving would
hurt so much. (Bombeck, *Family*, 2–3)

A friend of mine said, "A child loves his or her mother, but they
live for their father." Proverbs 17:6 reminds us, "The glory of children is
their fathers" (ESV).

Yes, daddies are important to the well-being of their children, but so
are their mothers. We live in a day when motherhood is not held in the
high esteem that it once was. Unfortunately, many women have mistak-
enly sacrificed the gift of motherhood and the joy of childbearing for a
career and other enticements that in the long run will never deliver the
joy and blessings that rearing children provides.

Several years ago someone sent me an article where one woman
is speaking to another. I doubt I have ever read anything that seemed
to capture in such a powerful fashion the greatness and importance of
motherhood. I think every woman who reads these words will probably
need a tissue at the end of the story.

It Will Change Your Life

Time is running out for my friend. While we are sitting at
lunch, she casually mentions that she and her husband are
thinking of "starting a family." What she means is that her

biological clock has begun its countdown, and she is being forced to consider the prospect of motherhood.

"We're taking a survey," she says half joking. "Do you think I should have a baby?"

"It will change your life," I say carefully, keeping my tone neutral.

"I know," she says. "No more spontaneous vacations . . ."

But that is not what I mean at all, and I try to decide what to tell her.

I want her to know what she will never learn in childbirth classes: that the physical wounds of childbearing heal, but that becoming a mother will leave an emotional wound so raw that she will be forever vulnerable.

I consider warning her that she will never read a newspaper again without asking "What if that had been my child?" That every plane crash, every fire will haunt her. That when she sees pictures of starving children, she will wonder if anything could be worse than watching your child die.

I look at her manicured nails and stylish suit and think that no matter how sophisticated she is, becoming a mother will reduce her to the primitive level of a bear protecting her cub. That an urgent call of "MOM!" will cause her to drop her best crystal without a moment's hesitation.

I feel I should warn her that no matter how many years she has invested in her career, she will be professionally derailed by motherhood. Oh, she might arrange for childcare, but one day she will be going into an important business meeting, and she will think about her baby's sweet smell. She will have to use every ounce of discipline to keep from running home, just to make sure her child is all right.

I want my friend to know that everyday decisions will no longer be routine. That a 5-year-old boy's desire to go to the men's restroom rather than the women's at a restaurant will become a major dilemma. That issues of independence and gender identity will be weighed against the prospect that a child molester may be lurking in that men's restroom. However decisive she may be at the office, she will second-guess herself constantly as a mother.

Looking at my attractive friend, I want to assure her that
eventually she will shed the pounds of pregnancy, but she
will never feel the same about herself. That her life now, so
important, will be of less value to her once she has a child.
That she would give it up in a moment to save her offspring,
but will also hope for more years—not to accomplish her own
dreams, but to watch her child accomplish his.

My friend's relationship with her husband will change,
but not in the ways she thinks. I wish she could understand
how much more you can love a man who is always careful to
powder the baby or who never hesitates to play with his son or
daughter. I think she should know that she will fall in love with
her husband all over again, but for reasons she would now
find very unromantic. . . .

I want to describe to my friend the exhilaration of seeing
your child learn to hit a baseball. I want to capture for her
the belly laugh of a baby who is touching the soft fur of a dog
for the first time. I want her to taste the joy that is so real, it
actually hurts.

My friend's quizzical look makes me realize that tears have
formed in my eyes. "You'll never regret it," I say finally. Then
reaching across the table, and squeezing my friend's hand, I
offer a silent prayer for her and me and all the mere mortal
women who stumble their way into this holiest of callings.
(Bourke, "Motherhood")

Practical Applications from Song of Songs 2:15

Let's draw our attention to one area where men and women are different: the area of sex. Repeatedly we need to do some good, hard thinking
about this good gift from our great God.

If only because one of them is a man and the other a woman, married couples usually have quite different attitudes and approaches to
sex. Furthermore, many people may come to marriage with varying
beliefs and expectations. Below is a tool[5] designed to open up discussion

---

[5] Adapted from *Sexual Fulfillment in Marriage: A Multimedia Learning Kit* by Clifford
and Joyce Penner, Family Concern, Inc., 1977.

about these differences. Take it with your spouse and see what you can learn about each other.

	Agree	Disagree	Uncertain
Sex is one of the most beautiful aspects of life.	____	____	____
In the act of sex, it is more enjoyable to give than to receive.	____	____	____
Bodily pleasure is fleshly and not spiritual and therefore wrong.	____	____	____
Sexual intercourse is primarily for physical release.	____	____	____
Our religious beliefs have significant influence on our attitudes toward sexual behavior.	____	____	____
Men and women have equal rights to sexual pleasure.	____	____	____

There are sexual activities that I would consider wrong for a married couple to practice. If you agree, list these: _____

_____

_____

	Agree	Disagree	Uncertain
To be truly satisfying, intercourse must lead to simultaneous orgasm.	____	____	____
Sexual fantasies are normal.	____	____	____
Masturbation (self-stimulation) is an acceptable means for sexual pleasure and release.	____	____	____
The male always should be the aggressor in sexual activity.	____	____	____
In general, women don't enjoy sex as much as men.	____	____	____
Men should be allowed more freedom in sexual behavior than women.	____	____	____
The quality of a sexual relationship is more than just physical pleasure.	____	____	____

How Does This Text Exalt Christ?

My Shepherd-King Builds and Cultivates Beautiful Vineyards

Men and women, husbands and wives, as we have seen over and over, are different by design. There is complementarity in a biblical marriage. There are also challenges. Sin puts stress on our relationship. Sometimes the "battle of the sexes" erupts. Women, in particular, are susceptible to emotional swings and outbursts. The life-changing power of the gospel, as they are being conformed to the image of Christ, is essential for their protection against the little foxes (Rom 8:29). A confidence that nothing can separate a wife from the love of Christ (Rom 8:35-39) is essential as she wages war against these little villains that only desire to harm her and her marriage.

This confidence in the love of her shepherd-king frees her to be a "woman of the Spirit." The fruit one finds in her vineyard is not immorality, impurity, idolatry, hatred, strife, jealousy, outbursts of anger, or selfish ambitions (Gal 5:19-20). No, the fruit we find in this "Eden regained and more" is love, joy, peace, patience, kindness, goodness, faith, gentleness, and self-control (Gal 5:22-23). These holy repellants send the little foxes scurrying. They flee the vineyard because they cannot abide by the fragrance of these gospel fruits.

Little foxes, little sins, are no match for the power of the gospel lived out by two spouses transformed by the grace of God. The love it gives is so great, "mighty waters cannot extinguish it" (Song 8:7), and little foxes cannot destroy it. The Christ-characteristics of 1 Corinthians 13:4-8 provide a protection that is other-worldly! These are wonderful verses to bring this study to a close:

> *Love is patient, love is kind. Love does not envy, is not boastful, is not conceited, does not act improperly, is not selfish, is not provoked, and does not keep a record of wrongs. Love finds no joy in unrighteousness but rejoices in the truth. It bears all things, believes all things, hopes all things, endures all things. Love never ends.*

This is the vineyard cultivated by my Shepherd-King-Bridegroom!

Reflect and Discuss

1. Why are gender differences especially prone to become "foxes" in a marriage?
2. What other passages of Scripture inform our communication? How can our communication be both a blessing and a curse?
3. Where in the Song do you see the couple cultivating romance? How do they do this?
4. What does it mean that men and women are hard-wired differently? How can you see in Song of Songs that Solomon and Shulammite are wired differently?
5. What are some things you are tempted to look at for your self-worth? How can your calling and identity as a man or woman help provide a corrective? How does the gospel realign our self-worth?
6. What other Bible texts speak of our relationship to time? How do we often fail to use our time according to biblical wisdom and command?
7. How have you seen the important roles that a mother and a father each have in the life of a child? How does each role reflect the character of God?
8. Answer the questions in the Practical Application section with your spouse and discuss the answers you each have. Where are there differences? How can these become dangerous "foxes"?
9. Identify some foxes that women are particularly susceptible to, and talk through how the gospel guards against these in a marriage.
10. Identify some foxes that men are particularly susceptible to, and talk through how the gospel guards against these in a marriage.

Is He Really the Man of My Dreams?

SONG OF SONGS 3:1-5

Main Idea: The right spouse is worth waiting for and searching after diligently. In the gospel, Jesus Himself seeks after His bride even when she is unworthy.

I. **Do You Really Love Him (3:1)?**
II. **Is He Worth the Risk (3:2-3)?**
III. **Is He the One With Whom You Want to Spend the Rest of Your Life (3:4)?**
IV. **Is He Worth the Wait (3:5)?**

The blessings and benefits of marriage are far too many to count. As two become one (Gen 2:24), the life experiences shared, involving both joy and pain, enrich our lives and make us better. At least they can and should.

This was beautifully illustrated to me some years ago when I came across a strangely titled article: "Berry Mauve or Muted Wine?" It is a powerful story of love, courage, and devotion forged in the hot flames of real life and covenant marriage.

Berry Mauve or Muted Wine?

He found me weeping bitterly in the hospital room. "What's wrong?" Richard asked, knowing we both had reason to cry. In the past 48 hours, I had discovered the lump in my breast was cancerous; the cancer had spread to my lymph nodes; and there was a possible spot on my brain.

I was 32 years old and the mother of three beautiful children. Richard pulled me tight and tried to comfort me. Many had expressed amazement at the peace that had overwhelmed me from the beginning. God was my comfort the moment before I found out I had cancer, and He remained the same after. But it seemed to Richard that all that had crashed in the few moments he had been out of the room.

He held me tight. "It's all been too much, hasn't it, Suz?" he said. "That's not it," I cried and held up the hand mirror I had found in the drawer. Richard was puzzled. "I didn't know it was like this," I cried. I had found the mirror in the nightstand and was shocked at my reflection. I didn't even recognize myself. After the surgery, I groaned in my sleep and well-meaning friends had freely pushed the self-dispensing medication to ease what they thought was pain. Unfortunately I was allergic to morphine and had swelled like a sausage. Betadine from the surgery stained my neck, shoulder, and chest and it was too soon for a bath.

A tube hung out of my side draining the fluid from the surgical site. My left shoulder and chest was wrapped tightly in gauze where I had lost a portion of my breast. My long, curly hair was matted into one big wad.

What hit me the hardest was that over 100 people had come to see me over the past 48 hours and they had all seen this brown and white, swollen, makeup-less, matted-haired, gray-gowned woman that used to be me. Where had I gone?

Richard left the room. Within moments he came back, his arms laden with small bottles. He pulled pillows out of the closet and dragged a chair over to the sink. He unraveled my IV and tucked the long tube from my side in his shirt pocket. He reached down and picked me up and scooted the IV stand with one foot as he carried me over to the chair. As he sat me down gently on his lap, he cradled my head in his arms over the sink and began to run warm water through my hair. He poured the small bottles he had confiscated from the cart in the hall over my hair and washed and conditioned my long curls. He wrapped my hair in a towel and he carried me, the tube and IV stand back over to the bed. All of this done so gently that not one stitch was disturbed.

My husband, who has never blow-dried his thick dark hair in his life, took out the blow drier and dried my hair, the whole while entertaining me as he pretended to give beauty tips. He then proceeded, with the experience of watching me for the past 12 years, to fix my hair. I laughed as he bit his lip, more serious than any beauty school student. He bathed my shoulder and neck with a warm washcloth, careful to not disturb the area around the surgery and rubbed lotion into my skin. Then he opened my makeup bag and began to apply makeup. I will never forget the laughter we shared as he tried to apply my mascara and blush. I opened my eyes wide and held my breath as his hands shook as he brushed the mascara on my lashes. He rubbed my cheeks with tissue to blend in the blush.

With the last touch, he held up two lipsticks. "Which one? Berry mauve or muted wine?" he asked. He applied the lipstick like an artist painting on a canvas and then held the little mirror in front of me. I was human again. A little swollen, but I smelled clean, my hair hung softly over my shoulders and I recognized who I was. "What do you think?" he asked. I began to cry again, this time because I was grateful. "No, baby. You'll mess up my makeup job," he said, and then I burst into laughter.

During this difficult time in our lives, I was given only a 10–40% chance of survival over five years. That was nine years ago. I made it through those years with laughter, with God's comfort, and with the help of a man brought into my life named Richard. We will celebrate our 21st anniversary this year with our three children—our twins, who are 17, and our 18-year-old daughter. Richard understood what others might have taken for vanity in the midst of tragedy. Everything I had ever taken for granted had been shaken in those hours—the fact that I would watch my children grow, my health, my future. With one small act of kindness, Richard gave me normalcy. I will always see that moment as one of the kindest gestures of our marriage. (Eller, "Berry Mauve," 26–28) [This was written in 1999. In January 2014 I corresponded with Suzanne. She is doing well!]

Song of Songs 3:1-5 appears to be a dream, or maybe better, a nightmare, that the bride-to-be had one night as her wedding day was approaching. Understandably there was excitement, but also anxiety. She was nervous. There were still some questions racing through her mind. Is this shepherd-king really the man of my dreams? Is he truly the one that I want to be with "till death do us part"? She is determined to find the answers and we can summarize the "search-and-find mission" she sets out on by raising four questions these verses will answer for us.

Do You Really Love Him?
SONG OF SONGS 3:1

Perhaps the king has returned to the city (3:3), leaving Shulammite alone in the country. Their separation is painful to her, but it is also helpful. It provides insight and it clarifies her true feelings. Four times in the poem she refers to the king as "the one I love" (3:1-4). The ESV translates it "whom my soul loves." We also see four times the theme of "seeking" (3:1-2). She is alone in bed struggling through a restless night. Once again he is absent (cf. 1:7), and she misses him badly. Why? Because she really does love this man. Her bed is where he belongs and she wants him there! This will happen soon, but not soon enough as far as she is concerned. She is seeking the one she loves but she cannot find him. This is a situation that must be remedied. This is a situation that she will not stand for. Richard Hess remarks, "The female's desire for her lover, equal in intensity to her desire to live, will cause her to go forth and seek him" (Hess, *Song*, 103).

Settle in your heart that you truly love the person you are considering for marriage. If there are doubts, then wait. If questions remain, then put things on hold. There is something worse than not being married: it is being married to the wrong person. Wisdom may sometimes say, "Wait," especially when it comes to matters of the heart.

Is He Worth the Risk?
SONG OF SONGS 3:2-3

Shulammite looked for her king but did not find him (3:1). She will now do something about it, risking both life and reputation in the process. She is convinced he is worth it. She leaves the comfort of her bed (though on this night it had been anything but comfortable!) and the safety of her home, venturing into the city (3:2). No doubt it is the capital city of Jerusalem (3:5) with its streets and plazas (ESV, "squares"). This statement adds weight to the interpretation that 3:1-5 is a dream sequence. Going out at night and alone is something a woman would not do in that era, or for that matter, in any era. This is especially true in the Middle East. Tom Gledhill says of her actions that they are "irrational, impractical, impossible" (*Message*, 144). However, her love for this man is so great she will risk it all. She will cast proper decorum to the wind as she seeks the one she loves.

Unfortunately, she again is met with disappointment: "I sought him, but did not find him." You can almost feel panic setting in. Her heart is pounding, her mind is racing. She cannot find him but suddenly she is found: "The guards [ESV, "watchmen"] who go about the city found me" (v. 3). The significance of the guards (cf. 5:7; Jer 6:17) is not readily evident. Certainly they are men of authority and importance. Could it also be that they are men who are wise in the way of the streets ("street smart") who could help our lady locate her man? Perhaps while on patrol they had seen the king. Regardless of the circumstances, she has only one question for these street cops, these highway patrolmen: "Have you seen the one I love?" She is bold and clear in her question. She is not hesitant, even with strangers, to profess her love and devotion to her man. Hers is a healthy (not reckless) abandonment in search of the one her soul, her very life, loves.

Over time, after they are married, it will continue to be a healthy sign of their relationship that they miss each other and long for each other when they are apart. After all, "the LORD God said, 'It is not good for the man to be alone'" (Gen 2:18). It is not good for the woman either. However, because their love will mature and deepen, a confidence and security will develop that will lay anxieties and fears to rest. That there would ever be a time that they would look forward to and actually enjoy being apart would be a telltale sign that their marriage was in serious trouble.

Is He the One With Whom You Want to Spend the Rest of Your Life?
SONG OF SONGS 3:4

This is the longest verse in our five-verse poem. It is also the happiest! Overtones of Mary Magdalene finding the risen Lord Jesus are in the air (John 20:11-18)! We will address that shortly.

In this dream sequence, the guards said nothing to Shulammite (v. 3), so she moves on. She will not be sidetracked or stopped as she seeks her king. Suddenly, unexpectedly, she tells us, "I had just passed them when I found the one I love." We can easily sense her excitement in her discovery! "I found him! I found him!"

Finding him, she is anything but docile and passive in her response: "I held on to him and would not let him go until I brought him to my mother's house—to the chamber of the one who conceived me."

Shulammite's persistence has paid off. She found her bridegroom-king and she is not about to let him go, now or ever. To make crystal clear her intentions, she takes him to her maternal home, a place where she feels safe and secure. Further, in beautiful Hebrew parallelism, she will take him into "the chamber of the one who conceived me." I believe this means she took him into the bedroom for a time of intimacy. Tremper Longman says, "She grabbed him ardently and pulled him back to the privacy of her mother's bedroom. These actions certainly dispel a typical stereotype of the woman's 'role' in a relationship. She is no passive wallflower waiting for the advances of the more active male. She grabs him and hauls him off to the privacy of the bedroom" (Longman, *Songs*, 130). Gledhill believes our text means even more than this! He notes,

> "The house of my mother" could be translated more exactly as "my mother-house," with the possessive "my" qualifying the compound unit "mother-house." Then "mother-house" could literally be the chamber where motherhood becomes a reality, that is, her womb. The phrase occurs again at 8:2 where again some intimate activity is implied (drinking spiced-wine, drinking from the juice of the girl's pomegranate), leading on to the embracing of 8:3 and the adjuration at 8:4. So again, motion to *my mother's house* leads us . . . metaphorically to the girl's own secret place, to the entrance to her womb, the "chamber" (1:4), the innermost sanctum of intimacy into which she longs to bring her lover. That this is the meaning is confirmed by the request the girl (or is it the author?) makes, that love should not be awakened or aroused until there is an appropriate opportunity for it to be fulfilled. Her dreamings have led her to explicit sexual fantasies, which cause her to be aroused, when there is no hope of satisfaction, except in the physical presence of *the one my heart loves*. But she is still alone, and her fantasies are an exercise in frustration, so it is better that she not be aroused at all. (Gledhill, *Message*, 145)

Such actions on the part of a woman or man should only take place when you are rock solid certain this is the person you want to spend the rest of your life with. Indeed such actions should only take place within the covenant of marriage, which leads us to our fourth and final question.

Is He Worth the Wait?
SONG OF SONGS 3:5

Verse 5 is the second of three occasions (2:7; 3:5; 8:4) in which the readers of this Song are placed under an oath along with the "Young women of Jerusalem" (NKJV, ESV, "O daughters of Jerusalem"). There is a divine solemnity to this oath as all are challenged to not give way to sexual passion "until the appropriate time." That time, as Scripture makes perfectly clear, is marriage between a man and a woman united in a covenant relationship for life. Indeed as King Jesus said in Matthew 19:6, "What God has joined together, man must not separate."

Once again we are reminded that sex is a good (great!) gift from a great God. What is necessary for its maximal enjoyment is the right person at the right place at the right time. Here there is maximum protection, pleasure, and partnership. If he is the right man, he is worth the wait. If she is the right woman, she is worth the wait.

Unfortunately, too many have been deceived by the lies of the evil one. They have been convinced that premarital sex is the norm and that it comes without consequences, and in their deception they have suffered disappointments and sorrows that are all too common. In their well-researched book *Premarital Sex in America* (2011), Mark Regnerus and Jeremy Uecker expose what they call "Ten Myths about Sex in Emerging America." These are especially relevant to the issue of sex before and outside of marriage and provide serious food for thought. These myths include:

- MYTH: Long-term relationships are a thing of the past.
- MYTH: Sex is necessary to maintain a struggling relationship.
- MYTH: Boys are sexual beings and cannot be expected to follow sexual norms.
- MYTH: You are entirely in charge of your own sexuality; others' decisions don't matter.
- MYTH: Others are having more sex than you.
- MYTH: Sex doesn't need to mean much.
- MYTH: Living together is a positive step towards marriage. (Adapted from Regnerus and Uecker, *Premarital Sex in America*, 236–50)

Myths deceive, but God's Word is a sure and certain guide. His counsel is always for our holiness. His wisdom is always for our good. If this is the right person, he or she is worth the wait. You will be glad you waited.

Practical Applications from Song of Songs 3:1-5

Asking questions, lots of questions, is a wise and good thing to do before getting married. We should ask good questions of each other and we should also seek the wisdom of family and friends who love us and have our best interest at heart. It is simply impossible to have too much information when we make this second most important decision we will ever make in all of life. Of course, the first and most important decision of all is whether I will trust my life completely and only to Jesus Christ as my personal Lord and Savior. No questions will ever trump this one!

Howard Hendricks (1924–2013) was a hero in ministry to me and thousands of others. "Prof," as he was fondly known by his students, taught Bible Interpretation at Dallas Theological Seminary for more than 50 years. But he also taught on marriage and family. Some years ago a friend passed on to me Prof's list of "Thirty Questions Most Frequently Asked by Young Couples Looking Forward to Marriage." There is some real wisdom here, and any couple contemplating marriage would be well served to walk through them one by one.

1. Where should a couple stop in petting before marriage?
2. Is jealously part of love for your mate?
3. Who should control the purse strings?
4. When both are working, is the wife's money hers or theirs? If both work, who should support the family while (if) the husband continues his schooling?
5. Is there any reason why the wife should not support the family while the husband continues his schooling?
6. Should the husband help with housework?
7. Should couples have a will drawn up soon after marriage?
8. Should a young couple carry insurance?
9. What are the effects of frequent business travel or unusual working hours on marital happiness?
10. To what extent should we discuss our pasts?
11. Is it true that people are not really "in love" until after they have been married for some years?
12. When we differ, how can we work out a happy adjustment?
13. Is it true that quarrels are never necessary?

14. If we come from divided families, can we profit by our parents' mistakes?
15. When we belong to two quite different churches, how do we work out our differences, and what about children?
16. How can a couple keep in-laws in their place but still make them feel loved and necessary?
17. What if he feels she does not give enough and she feels he does not give enough, they talk about it and still feel this way—what is suggested?
18. How soon after marriage should a couple plan to have children?
19. When considering having children, should the decision be primarily economic?
20. Are contraceptives safe to use? Do they lead to cancer or sterility? [Possibly abortion?]
21. What part does each spouse have in the love play preceding and during intercourse?
22. Is every couple able to have satisfactory intercourse?
23. Is it harmful or wrong to have intercourse during menstruation?
24. Is there danger of constantly arousing sexual desires and not fulfilling this desire, in both male and female?
25. How does a woman know when she reaches a climax?
26. Do women undergo emotional changes during pregnancy and menstrual periods?
27. How important is it for couples to know their RH factor?
28. Are regular times for prayer important?
29. Are there occasions in marriage when divorce seems a reasonable and even proper solution?
30. If we find difficulties arising in our marriage what immediate steps should we take?

How Does This Text Exalt Christ?

I Will Seek My King

Douglas O'Donnell draws our attention to the fact that "there is a long history of Christians making a connection between the heart of our text (3:1-4) and John 20, the tomb scene where Mary Magdalene encountered the resurrected Jesus. Hippolytus (Bishop of Rome from 222 to 235), was the first to point out the possible parallels between the Song and this Gospel scene, arguing that our text is a prophecy" (O'Donnell, *Song*, 71). It is indeed the case that both Shulammite and Mary go in search of their king while it is dark. Both are met by others in their search. Both, once finding the object of their affection, cling fast, not wanting to ever let go again. These parallels are worth thinking about to be sure.

O'Donnell also notes certain thematic elements with another well-known Gospel story: the story of the wee little man named Zacchaeus (Luke 19:1-10). Again we see a man seeking the King, finding Him, and taking Him to his house! This is good! But—and I appreciate O'Donnell's insight so much at this point—this little story is eclipsed by the "Big Story" of redemption:

> But wait. Zacchaeus sought and found Jesus. That's the story. True, he did. But Jesus sought and found Zacchaeus—that's the bigger story [Luke 19:10]. Jesus came out of his safe home to seek after sinners like Zacchaeus, people who are lost in the city streets and squares, and to bring them home to the security and intimacy of his love. (O'Donnell, *Song*, 72)

So Jeremiah 29:13-14 most certainly is true and beautifully illustrated in Song of Songs 3:1-5: "You will seek Me and find Me when you search for Me with all your heart. I will be found by you—this is the Lord's declaration." Yes, we will find our King when we seek Him, but unlike Shulammite, it will be because He first sought us, He first loved us (1 John 4:19). The Song of Songs is a beautiful love story to be sure. And it is a door that opens up to us an even greater love story, the greatest love story of all, found in a greater King, a greater Solomon, the King whose name is Jesus.

Reflect and Discuss

1. Why is it wise to settle doubts about love before a couple gets married?
2. Why is it healthy for a man and a woman to miss one another when absent? How does this reflect the gospel?
3. Why should we expect that a couple's confidence in their marriage will develop over time and alleviate anxiety when they are apart? What's the difference between missing someone and being fearful or anxious when they are away?

4. Shulammite searches and dreams with great intensity about the one she loves. Why should such feelings and thoughts be reserved for the one with whom we are committed to spending our life?

5. Discuss the similarities between Shulammite's seeking after Solomon and the psalmist's seeking in Psalm 27. What other psalms reflect such urgent longing?

6. Discuss the importance of reserving sex for "the right person at the right place at the right time." How do you define each of these? How does the Bible?

7. Why does it make sense to wait for sex, if you know you have found "the right person"? How is the biblical view on this issue different from popular culture?

8. If you are engaged, talk through the list of 30 questions in this chapter. Which are the ones you need to talk through further and seek guidance in answering?

9. Discuss the parallels between this text and John 20, Luke 19, and Jeremiah 29:13-14.

10. Why is it good news that Jesus seeks us, even as we seek to see Him (cf. Zacchaeus in Luke 19)?

The Return of the King!
(What a Great Day for a Wedding)

SONG OF SONGS 3:6-11

Main Idea: Great weddings will reflect important components of the gospel and anticipate the day when Jesus returns for His bride, the church.

I.   A Great Wedding Will Involve a Public Celebration (3:6-7).
II. A Great Wedding Contains a Promise of Protection (3:7-8).
III. A Great Wedding Includes a Pledge of Love (3:9-10).
IV. A Great Wedding Has the Approval of Others (3:11).

I believe the most important decision a person will ever make in life is whether or not they will personally trust Jesus Christ as their Lord and Savior. He lived the life (a perfect, sinless life) we all should have lived but didn't. He died the death (as a penal substitute bearing in our place the wrath and just judgment of God) we should have died. And He offers us a free gift (eternal life) we do not deserve. The great King from heaven came "to seek and to save the lost" (Luke 19:10), and He will save anyone who comes to Him in repentance and faith.

Now there is another decision that I believe clearly ranks second in importance to the first. It is the question, "Whom will I marry and make a covenant to spend the rest of my life with?" I believe this question is so important that I require all prospective couples I consider marrying to sign off on a "Premarital Wedding Covenant." This requirement is not negotiable. Sign it and I will consider performing your marriage ceremony. Refuse to sign it and I refuse to do your wedding. Here is the premarital covenant that I place before them.

Premarital Wedding Covenant

The decision to marry is the second most important decision one will ever make in a lifetime. The first is the decision whether or not you will personally commit your life to Jesus Christ as Savior and Lord. Keeping this in mind, we commit to God, our minister, and each other to:

1. Seek God's will for our lives personally and together by following biblical principles for Christian living and marriage.
2. Not engage in premarital sex or any inappropriate sexual activity.
3. Be sure to do everything possible to build a Christian marriage and home. This means that both of us have a personal relationship with Jesus Christ, and that we desire growth for that relationship over the entire course of our lives by being obedient to his Word.
4. Read and listen to all pre-marital material provided by our minister. These materials are available at no cost at http://danielakin.com.
5. Be active together in a Bible-believing church beginning now and during our marriage.
6. Buy and read *His Needs, Her Needs* by Willard Harley, *The Act of Marriage* by Tim LaHaye, *God on Sex* by Danny Akin, and *A Promise Kept* by Robertson McQuilkin.
7. Maintain total openness and honesty with our minister and with each other both now and after our wedding.
8. Postpone or cancel the marriage if, at any time between now and the wedding, either one of us comes to believe this marriage is not right.
9. Never allow the word *divorce* to enter the realm of our relationship. We are in this together for the duration of our lives. Divorce is not an option for us!
10. Seek competent Christian counsel should we encounter any difficulty in our marriage, beginning with the minister who performs our wedding.

With the above commitments made, we believe God will be honored and the prospects for a meaningful and happy marriage enhanced. With God's help, we will seek to honor God with our lives and marriage all the days of our lives.

Man's Signature   _____

Woman's Signature_____

Shulammite has suffered a bad dream, a nightmare (3:1-5). Apparently Solomon had returned to the city (3:2-3) and left her alone in the countryside (2:8-17). In her dream she went in search of "the one I love" (3:1-4) and found him (3:4). They were united and she was determined not to let him go (3:4). Her dream will now give way to reality as she is reunited with her shepherd-king. And she is not the one who goes after him! No, her man is coming after her with a royal wedding entourage. The days of courting have come to an end. The time for their marriage is at hand (3:6-11). The celebration of their wedding night is soon to follow (4:1–5:1). It is the right time to stir up and awaken the intimacies of lovemaking!

Thomas Constable informs us,

> Weddings in Israel took place in front of the local town elders, not the priests (e.g., Ruth 4:10-11). They transpired in homes, not in the tabernacle or temple (or synagogue, in later times). They were civil rather than religious ceremonies.
>
> There were three parts to a wedding in the ancient Near East. First, the groom's parents selected a bride for their son. This involved securing the permission of the bride's parents and the approval of both the bride and the groom themselves. Though the parents of the young people arranged the marriage, they usually obtained the consent of both the bride and the groom. Second, on the wedding day the groom proceeded to the bride's house accompanied by a group of friends. He then escorted her to the site of the wedding ceremony, and finally took her to their new residence accompanied by their friends. Physical union consummated the marriage the night after the wedding ceremony took place. Third, the couple feasted with their friends—usually for seven days following the wedding ceremony. (Constable, "Notes")[6]

From these six verses, four truths emerge that help us see and understand certain characteristics that should accompany every wedding ceremony that our great God has planned for those who long to honor Him in this sacred, covenantal union. It is a beautiful and fantastic scene that unfolds before us.

A Great Wedding Will Involve a Public Celebration
SONG OF SONGS 3:6-7

Our love song suddenly shifts scenes. It moves from the private to the public. It is the day of Shulammite's wedding to her shepherd-king! The

---

[6] Constable draws from an article by Edwin M. Yamauchi, "Cultural Aspects of Marriage in the Ancient World," *BibSac* 135 (1978): 241–52.

author of the Song takes the posture of a narrator in verses 6-11. The unfolding scene is majestic as Solomon comes for his bride in this wedding processional. Jack Deere points out,

> The pomp and beauty of this procession were wholly appropriate in light of the event's significance. The Scriptures teach that marriage is one of the most important events in a person's life. Therefore it is fitting that the union of a couple be commemorated in a special way. The current practice of couples casually living together apart from the bonds of marriage demonstrates how unfashionable genuine commitment to another person has become in contemporary society. This violates the sanctity of marriage and is contrary to God's standards of purity. (Deere, "Song," 1017)

The text says the king is "coming up from the wilderness." The theme of the wilderness is a rich one in the Old Testament and immediately evokes the ideas of the exodus, wandering, difficulty, and hardship. The wilderness reminds us that the ravaging effects of the curse are ever present in this fallen world and that the most precious and tender relationships are not immune to its influences. Elijah (1 Kgs 19), John the Baptist (Matt 3:1-5), and King Jesus (Matt 4:1-11) also had wilderness experiences. But God was faithful, as He was with Israel, to sustain them and provide for them. This is what our Lord intends for marriage as well.

Shulammite had lived through a number of difficult and trying experiences, wilderness experiences (1:6-8; 3:1-3). Now, however, those days are over as her bridegroom-king comes in full display for all to see to fetch her as his wife! What appears to be "columns of smoke" are the sweet scents of "myrrh and frankincense," exotic spices imported from places like Arabia and India (Longman, *Song*, 135). From Shulammite's perspective, as well as that of the audience watching this scene unfold, things look good and they smell good. Solomon makes a full public display of his love and affection for his bride and he invites all who are there to join in this celebration.

In Matthew 2:11 we read that when the Magi saw the baby Jesus, they fell to their knees and worshiped Him. They then gave Him gifts of gold, frankincense, and myrrh. Why? Because these were gifts fitting for a king! Solomon is not only going to make Shulammite a queen, he is going to treat her like a queen. Privately (4:1-16) and publicly, he will honor her and cherish her as God did Israel and as Christ does His church (Eph 5:25-33).

Unfortunately, Israel would forget the Lord "who brought us from the land of Egypt, who led us through the wilderness, through a land of deserts and ravines, through a land of drought and darkness, a land no one traveled through and where no one lived" (Jer 2:6). This shepherd-king publically pledges that this bride will never again find herself in the wilderness as he takes her to be his wife. We have a Shepherd-King named Jesus who promises us the same! And what is His public pledge? A Roman cross and an empty Judean tomb!

A Great Wedding Contains a Promise of Protection
SONG OF SONGS 3:7-8

As this scene unfolds we receive greater clarity in verses 7-8. The vision of the columns of smoke that are the burning of "myrrh and frankincense from every fragrant powder of the merchant" (no expense was spared) is now revealed to be "Solomon's royal litter [carriage]." And it is "surrounded by 60 warriors from the mighty of Israel," twice the number that accompanied King David (2 Sam 23:13-39). These are elite soldiers, Navy Seals, Army Rangers—his personal bodyguards who are armed and ready for action at any time. How do we know these soldiers are elite? First, they are "warriors from the mighty of Israel." Second, "All of them are skilled with swords and trained in warfare." Third, "Each has his sword at his side to guard against the terror of the night." Shulammite felt alone and unprotected at night in 3:1, but that will never happen again under the watchful care and protection of her shepherd-king and his mighty resources.

These royal bodyguards are a pledge and promise of protection that will accompany their marriage until death separates them. These groomsmen are his closest and most trusted confidants. He can trust his life or wife into their care with no fear. Even at night, when evil men come out to do evil things, she will be safe and secure.

In a sermon on this text, Mark Driscoll is quite practical in what a godly husband will promise and provide for his bride:

> He's looking out for her safety and her well-being, and this
> is something that a man has the great opportunity to do with
> the woman that he loves. In our day, this would include: safe
> car, living in a place that is safe and well-lit and not dangerous
> and crime-infested. This would include: wife gets a cell phone
> so that if emergency comes, she can contact you, you're

accessible and available. This would also include things like medical insurance, life insurance, so that even in the occasion of your death you're still providing for her and/or your children. He's a man who thinks through issues of safety and protection. Provision: He's coming to pick her up. 60 warriors carrying her into town: enormous wedding day. The kind of wedding day that little girls dress up like princesses for, and practice, beginning at a very young age for this kind of amazing wedding day. (Driscoll, "His Garden")

And in the context of the wedding ceremony itself, Tommy Nelson is right on target when he writes,

Part of the safety and security of the wedding ceremony will be evident in the people who serve as your best man, maid or matron of honor, groomsmen, and bridesmaids. Choose godly people who will support you fully in the vows you make. As a whole, those who witness your marriage should be like a holy hedge of protection around you, keeping you focused toward each other inside the circle of matrimony, and keeping out anybody who might try to destroy your marriage. Don't ask someone to stand up for you who isn't completely committed to you, to your marriage, and in general, to the sanctity and value of marriage. Such a person will not encourage you to work through problems in your marriage. Such a person will not do the utmost to help you and your spouse when you need help. And they may embarrass you at the rehearsal dinner! (Nelson, *Book of Romance*, 76)

A Great Wedding Includes a Pledge of Love
SONG OF SONGS 3:9-10

When it comes to the popular arrangement of cohabitation, there is an important "C" word that is missing: commitment. It also is sad to note that more and more modern wedding ceremonies are dropping the phrase "till death do us part" for more cautious and tentative promises like "for as long as our marriage shall serve the common good" (Harlow, "Bride's Vow"). Other phrases showing up more often include "I promise to be loyal as long as love lasts" and "until our time together is over."

Marriage as designed by God involves a lifelong commitment to covenantal love. There is a pledge and promise of physical, spiritual, emotional, and personal commitment that only God brings to an end. We see this kind of commitment put on public display in verses 9-10 in the wedding carriage (HCSB, "sedan chair"; marginal reading is "palanquin") "King Solomon made for himself." This "carriage" or "sedan chair" was made of the very best materials money could buy. The wood was "from Lebanon." The timbers from these forests were in great demand throughout the ancient Near East (Carr, *Song*, 111). It was from this wood that Solomon had carved his sedan chair or carriage. Added to this were "posts of silver," supports of gold, and a "seat of purple." All of this was exquisitely beautiful and expensive. It was Solomon's way of saying, "I will keep nothing back from you. All I have now belongs to you. You will always receive my best."

Verse 10 also informs us that the carriage's "interior is inlaid with love by the young women of Jerusalem." The phrase "inlaid with love" is vague and even mysterious, and "the young women of Jerusalem" provide a female counterpart to the "mighty warriors" of verses 7-8. What are we to make of all of this? Commentators go in many different directions trying to unwrap the verse's meaning, so dogmatism in interpretation is certainly out of bounds. I do find helpful and attractive the comments of the great Baptist preacher in London, Charles Spurgeon. He states that the phrase

> is a complicated, but very expressive form of speech. Some regard the expression as signifying a pavement of stone, engraved with hieroglyphic emblems of love, which made up the floor of this travelling chariot; but this would surely be very uncomfortable and unusual, and therefore others have explained the passage as referring to choice embroidery and dainty carpets, woven with cost and care, with which the interior of the travelling-chair was lined. Into such embroidery sentences of love-poetry may have been worked. Needlework was probably the material of which it was composed; skillful fingers would therein set forth emblems and symbols of love. As the spouse in the second chapter sings, "His banner over me was love," probably alluding to some love-word upon the banner; so, probably, tokens of love were carved or embroidered, as the case may have been, upon the interior of the chariot, so that "the midst thereof was paved with love,

for the daughters of Jerusalem." We need not, however, tarry
long over the metaphor, but endeavor to profit by its teaching.
(Spurgeon, *Most Holy Place*, 281)

I believe we are on safe ground to affirm that the phrase speaks clearly to
the truth that love will be their promise and pledge to each other from
their wedding day until their death day. John Phillips says the phrase
"suggests all that is romantic" (*Exploring*, 81). I would add, it suggests all
that one person commits to another in covenantal marriage. Love, not
lust, will be our circle of protection. Love, not infatuation, will be our
companion for life. A Christ-honoring wedding is just the right place
to make such a promise. Indeed, it is exactly the right place to make a
pledge to love another for life. Such love finds beautiful expression in
Song of Songs 8:5-14. It is wonderfully described by the apostle Paul in
1 Corinthians 13:4-8.

A Great Wedding Has the Approval of Others
SONG OF SONGS 3:11

The wedding of this great shepherd-king is the occasion of great celebration and rejoicing (cf. Ps 45). The "daughters of Jerusalem," also
known as "the young women of Jerusalem" (3:10), now called "the
young women of Zion," are commanded to "come out" and "gaze," look
intently on, "King Solomon wearing the crown his mother [Bathsheba]
placed on him the day of his wedding," a day that is called "the day of
his heart's rejoicing."

This day was truly different from his mother Bathsheba's wedding
day. She had been seduced into an adulterous affair by King David
and become pregnant (2 Sam 11:1-5). David then murdered her husband Uriah to cover up his sin (2 Sam 11:14-16). She would mourn his
death, and then be taken by David in marriage (2 Sam 11:26-27). The
Scriptures record no fanfare or celebration. It is one of the saddest and
most sordid stories in all of the Bible.

This day is different. Bathsheba can applaud this union and so can
everyone else. This marriage is right and this couple is right for each
other. The young women of Zion join in the celebration of the wedding.
Their friends say, "We approve of this marriage." In their minds this is a
good and wonderful thing that is about to happen. They like Solomon
when he is with Shulammite. She brings out the best in him, not the
worst, when they are together. The same is true for Shulammite. She is

a better and more beautiful woman when she is with her shepherd-king. This mutual improvement is a phenomenon that all of us should look for when choosing a spouse.

Solomon's mother and his family also approve. The potential for in-law problems does not loom over this wedding, as is too often the case. She had prepared for him a crown similar to an Olympian laurel wreath, which symbolized the gladness and joy of his wedding day. According to Rabbinic tradition, crowns were worn by bridegrooms and brides until the destruction of Jerusalem in AD 70 (Snaith, *Song*, 57). This was a day of happiness not only for the king and his queen, but for all who shared in this wonderful event. Those who most loved Solomon and Shulammite were confident this marriage was meant to be and meant to last. Their approval is no guarantee, but it is an indication of the confidence both family and friends had in the rightness of this union. This is something every wise couple will carefully consider as they work to have a great wedding and a great marriage. We all need friends and family in our corner praying for us and pulling for us.

Practical Applications from Song of Songs 3:6-11

When the red hot passions of desire are ablaze, we can easily confuse a thing called *lust* with a thing called *love*. This is especially true when we are young and the hormones are raging with desires wanting (even demanding!) to be satisfied. This is a time when "cooler heads" must prevail. This is a time when we need to see the mammoth difference between passing lust and lasting love. Dennis Rigstad is very helpful in his article, "Is It Love or Lust?" It is balanced, but best of all, it is biblical. Think through his observations. There is real wisdom here as we consider the person with whom we want to spend the rest of our life.

Lust

1. Focuses on self

   You have been called to liberty; only do not use liberty as an opportunity for the flesh. (Gal 5:13 NKJV)

2. Leads to frustration

   You want something, but don't get it. You kill and covet, but you cannot have what you want. (Jas 4:2 NIV 1984)

3. Continually wants more

   They are separated from the life of God . . . and have given
   themselves over to sensuality so as to indulge in every kind of
   impurity, with a continual lust for more. (Eph 4:18-19 NIV 1984)

4. Enslaves self

   To whom you present yourselves slaves to obey, you are that
   one's slaves . . . you have presented your members as slaves to
   uncleanness, and lawlessness. (Rom 6:16,19 NKJV)

5. Desires to gratify the sinful nature with things contrary to the Spirit

   The sinful nature desires what is contrary to the Spirit. (Gal 5:17
   NIV 1984)

   The acts of the sinful nature are obvious; sexual immorality,
   impurity and debauchery; idolatry and witchcraft; hatred, discord,
   jealousy, fits of rage, selfish ambition, dissensions, factions and
   envy; drunkenness, orgies and the like. (Gal 5:19-21 NIV 1984)

6. Excludes Christ

   Since they did not think it worthwhile to retain the knowledge of
   God, He gave them over to a depraved mind . . . they have become
   filled with every kind of wickedness, evil, greed and depravity.
   (Rom 1:28-29 NIV 1984)

7. Sins to gratify the desires

   All of us also lived among them at one time, gratifying the cravings
   of our sinful nature and following its desires and thoughts. (Eph
   2:3 NIV 1984)

8. Entices with evil desires

   But each one is tempted when, by his own evil desire, he is dragged
   away and enticed. (Jas 1:14 NIV 1984)

9. Wars against the soul

   I urge you, as aliens and strangers in the world, to abstain from
   sinful desires, which war against your soul. (1 Pet 2:11 NIV 1984)

10. Avoids commitment and leads to tragedy

    Don't lust for their beauty. Don't let their coyness seduce you. For a
    prostitute will bring a man to poverty, and an adulteress may cost
    him his very life. (Prov 6:25-26 LB)

Love

1. Focuses on the other

   Let each of you look not only for his own interests, but also for the interests of others. (Phil 2:4 NKJV)

2. Leads to fulfillment

   To know the love of Christ which passes knowledge; that you may be filled with all the fullness of God . . . who is able to do exceedingly abundantly above all that we ask or think, according to the power that works in us. (Eph 3:19-20 NKJV)

3. Brings satisfaction

   No discipline seems pleasant . . . Later on, however, it produces a harvest of righteousness and peace for those who have been trained by it. (Heb 12:11 NIV 1984)

4. Encourages self-control

   I discipline my body and bring it into subjection. (1 Cor 9:27 NKJV)

5. Desires to live by the Spirit

   Live by the Spirit, and you will not gratify the desires of the sinful nature. (Gal 5:16 NIV 1984)

6. Includes Christ

   Clothe yourselves with the Lord Jesus Christ, and do not think about how to gratify the desires of the sinful nature. (Rom 13:14 NIV 1984)

7. Seeks God to gain its desires

   Delight yourself in the Lord and He will give you the desires of your heart. (Ps 37:4 NIV 1984)

8. Prevents sin

   Love your neighbor as yourself. But if you bite and devour one another, beware lest you be consumed by one another! (Gal 5:14-15 NKJV)

9. Nourishes the soul

   May God Himself, the God of peace, sanctify you through and through. May your whole spirit, soul and body be kept blameless. (1 Thess 5:23 NIV 1984)

10. Commits to one another (free love is a contradiction of terms)

You, brethren, have been called to liberty; only do not use liberty as an opportunity for the flesh, but by love serve one another. (Gal 5:13 NKJV)

(Rigstad, "Is It Love or Lust?")

How Does This Text Exalt Christ?

Looking Forward to the Return of the King

Song of Songs 3:6-11 is about a shepherd-king coming for his beautiful virgin bride. He comes with his armies and he is wearing a crown fit for the occasion. It is a magnificent scene to be sure, but it pales in comparison to the wedding processional it anticipates, a wedding processional described in Revelation 19 when King Jesus, the Shepherd-King greater than David or Solomon, returns from Heaven to get his bride, his wife (Rev 19:7). He will not come up from the wilderness, with the memories of the fall and the deliverance of the exodus occupying our minds. No, He will descend from heaven riding a white horse. On His head will not be a simple crown, but many diadems because He is the "King of kings and Lord of lords" (Rev 19:12,16). The armies of heaven will accompany this Bridegroom (Rev 19:14) and He will shepherd the nations "with an iron scepter" (Rev 19:15).

Song of Songs 3:6-11 stirs our hearts for another wedding day that will consummate all of human history! There we will celebrate the marriage of the Lamb that was slain to His bride whom He purchased with His own blood (Rev 5:9-10). On that day, as Jonathan Edwards so eloquently wrote,

The church shall be brought to the full enjoyment of her bridegroom, having all tears wiped away from her eyes; and there shall be no distance or absence. She shall then be brought to the entertainments of an eternal wedding feast, and to dwell forever with her bridegroom; yea, to dwell eternally in his embraces. Then Christ will give her his loves; and she shall drink her fill, yea, she shall swim in the ocean of his love. (Edwards, "The Church's Marriage," 22)

"Wedding Day"

There's a stirring in the throne room
And all creation holds its breath
Waiting now to see the Bridegroom
Wondering how the bride will dress
And she wears white
And she knows that she's undeserving
She bears the shame of history
But this worn and weary maiden
Is not the bride that He sees
And she wears white head to toe
But only He can make it so

Chorus:
When someone dries your tears
When someone wins your heart
And says you're beautiful
When you don't know you are
And all you long to see
Is written on His face
Love has come and finally set you free
On that wedding day
On that wedding day

She has danced in golden castles
And she has crawled through beggar's dust
But today she stands before Him
And she wears His righteousness
And she will be who He adores
And this is what He made her for

(Chorus)

When the hand that bears the only scars
In Heaven touch her face
And the last tears she'll ever cry
Are finally wiped away
And the clouds roll back as He takes her hand
And walks her through the gates
Forever we will reign

(Chorus) (Mark Hall, Nichole Nordeman, Bernie Herms,
     "Wedding Day")[7]

Reflect and Discuss

1. Discuss the "most important question" and "second most important question" at the beginning of this chapter. Do you agree or disagree? Why?
2. Discuss the wilderness theme that runs throughout Scripture and how it plays into the life and ministry of Jesus. How does this theme relate to our text in this chapter?
3. What is significant about the public nature of a wedding celebration?
4. What kind of protection does Solomon provide for Shulammite? How can husbands provide protection for their wives today?
5. What aspect of the gospel is lost when a lifetime of love is not promised at a wedding? What passages of Scripture would you consult to argue for a lifetime of love?
6. Why is it important to have a community around us as we enter into and grow in our marriages? What other biblical passages might suggest the benefit of such a community?
7. Discuss the difference between love and lust. How do we know Solomon is truly in love with Shulammite? How can you make sure to cultivate love for your spouse, rather than lust?
8. How does this scene in the Song reflect Revelation 19? How is it different?
9. The wedding of Solomon and Shulammite prefigures the wedding of Christ to His bride, the church. How can we conduct our weddings to do the same?
10. What weddings have you been a part of that pointed to the final return of the great Shepherd-King? Discuss the power that weddings have in communicating the gospel to non-believers.

The Beauty and Delights
of the Christian Bedroom

SONG OF SONGS 4:1–5:1

Main Idea: By God's design, sexual intimacy is meant for the marriage bed and is to be kept pure, so that in its fullness it brings joy to the couple and reflects the purity of Christ's love for His Church.

I. **Express Your Love for Your Mate (4:1-7).**
   A. A godly husband will bless his wife with his words (4:1-7).
   B. A godly wife will bless her husband with her body (4:1-7).

II. **Express Your Desire for Your Mate (4:8-11).**
   A. Invitation: I want you (4:8).
   B. Captivation: There is no one like you (4:9-11).

III. **Express Your Availability to Your Mate (4:12-16).**
   A. Save yourself for your mate (4:12).
   B. Give yourself to your mate (4:13-15).

IV. **Express Your Satisfaction in Your Mate (4:16–5:1).**
   A. There is human satisfaction in marital consummation (4:16–5:1).
   B. There is divine satisfaction in marital consummation (5:1).

In an article titled "What They Didn't Teach You About Sex in Sunday School," Peggy Fletcher Stack writes, "Many people assume the Bible has just one message about sex: Don't do it" ("What They Didn't Teach"). Anyone who says that obviously has not read the Bible. God, in His Word, has a lot to say about sex and much of it is good. Indeed, God is pro-sex when it is enjoyed His way and for His glory. Yes, God should be glorified when we engage in the act of sex.

Sex as God designed it is good, exciting, intoxicating, powerful, and unifying. The Bible is not a book on sex, but it does contain a complete theology of sexuality: the purposes for sex, warnings against its misuse, and a beautiful picture of ideal physical and spiritual intimacy as set forth in the Song of Songs. The "one-flesh" relationship (cf. Gen 2:24) is the most intense physical intimacy and the deepest spiritual unity possible between a husband and wife. God always approves of this relationship in which a husband and wife meet each other's physical needs in sexual intercourse (cf. Prov 5:15-21).

Paul indicates that sexual activity in marriage can affect the Christian life, especially prayer (cf. 1 Cor 7:5). Both husband and wife have definite and equal sexual needs and responsibilities, which are to be met in marriage (1 Cor 7:3), and each is to strive to meet the needs of the other and not their own (Phil 2:3-5). Our great God gave us this good gift of sex for several important reasons, including (1) knowledge (cf. Gen 4:1), (2) intimate oneness (Gen 2:24), (3) comfort (Gen 24:67), (4) the creation of life (Gen 1:28), (5) play and pleasure (Song 2:8-17; 4:1-16), and (6) avoidance of temptation (1 Cor 7:2-5). There is maximum pleasure, protection, purity, and partnership in married sex between a man and a woman.

A husband is commanded to find satisfaction (Prov 5:19) and joy (Eccl 9:9) in his wife and only in his wife. And he is to concern himself with meeting her specific needs (Deut 24:5; 1 Pet 3:7). A wife also has responsibilities. These include (1) availability (1 Cor 7:3-5), (2) preparation and planning (Song 4:9-11), (3) interest (Song 4:16; 5:2), and (4) sensitivity to specific masculine needs (Gen 24:67). The feeling of oneness experienced by husband and wife in the physical, sexual union should remind both partners of the even more remarkable oneness that the spirit of a man or a woman experiences with God in spiritual new birth through faith in Jesus Christ (John 3). The union of husband and wife is to provide a picture to the watching world of that spiritual union of Christ the bridegroom and the Church His bride (Eph 5:22-33).[8]

There is beauty and blessing in the Christian bedroom. Here God says, "Eat, friends! Drink, be intoxicated with love!" (5:1). We have arrived at the wedding night. The bride and groom are alone with only God as the unseen but welcome guest. Here the couple consummates their marriage in intimate sexual union. Our passage, in exquisite poetry, provides for us a portrait of what a Christian bedroom should be. This is a return to the garden of Eden and the promised land God provides for those who love and trust Him. What are the activities God desires to take place when a husband and wife are alone in the marriage bed? We make four overarching observations from this awesome text.

---

[8] Much of this introduction is drawn from Daniel Akin, *God on Sex: The Creator's Ideas about Love, Intimacy, and Marriage* (Nashville: B&H, 2003), 136–37, which is adapted from "Notes on Song of Solomon 3:4-5" in *The Believer's Study Bible*, 912.

Express Your Love for Your Mate
SONG OF SONGS 4:1-7

These verses are a song of admiration spoken by our shepherd-king to his bride. They are alone in the bridal suite. The time for the sexual consummation of their marriage has arrived, but this will not happen until verse 16. True romance is an "environment of affection" in which sexual union will occur more often and with greater satisfaction. In other words, some essential preliminaries must precede the main event. Unfortunately, this is not always clear, especially to a male. Having been aroused sexually, a man is now on the prowl as a predator, and his bride can certainly feel the part of prey. Our shepherd-king was sensitive to this temptation, and so he begins with the most important sex organ we have: the brain! Thinking about how his new wife might feel, he wisely cultivates an atmosphere of love, safety, and affection through carefully chosen words.

A Godly Husband Will Bless His Wife with His Words (Song 4:1-7)

Three times, from the beginning to the end of this section, the king tells his queen that she is "beautiful." He tells her she is "beautiful, very beautiful" in verse 1. He says she is "absolutely beautiful" in verse 7, "with no imperfection in you." Twice he calls her his "darling" (4:1,7). In his eyes she is the perfect woman for him. She is his "standard of beauty." Mark Driscoll shares some valuable words of wisdom in this context:

> This is why we tell you, "Don't cohabitate. Don't fornicate. Don't look at pornography. Don't create a standard of beauty that is not your spouse and then compare your spouse to the standard of beauty. Have your spouse be your standard of beauty." This is the biblical principle: one-woman man; the Bible's against lust; those kinds of things. If she is his standard of beauty, then there is no flaw in her because she looks like her. He is not comparing her to other women, and the same is true for both husbands and wives. Your standard of beauty is your spouse. There is not a standard of beauty that you evaluate your spouse by. This is one of the great devastating effects of pornography. You lust after people, compare your spouse to them. It's impossible to be satisfied in your marriage if you don't have a standard that is biblical. The standard is always your spouse. (Driscoll, "His Garden")

Women are verbal creatures. They are moved by what they hear and by what they feel. Tommy Nelson notes, "To a great extent, she thinks and feels [about herself] the way a man leads her to think and feel" (*Book of Romance*, 89). A man must learn to touch her heart (her mind) through her ear. This helps her feel good about herself in a God-intended way. It relaxes her, prepares her, and motivates her to give herself in passionate lovemaking to her husband. A wise man will understand the value of words, the right words, in preparation for sexual intimacy.

A study in *Psychology Today* noted that women are more likely to be disappointed with marriage than men, especially in the context of romance. Why?

> One explanation is that as compared with men, they have higher expectations for intimacy, and thus react more negatively to conjugal reality. In a major national survey more wives than husbands said that they wished their spouse talked more about thoughts and feelings, and more wives felt resentment and irritation with husbands than vice versa. The researchers conclude: In marriage . . . women talk and want verbal responsiveness of the kind they have had with other women, but their men are often silent partners, unable to respond in kind. (Rubenstein, "Modern Art," 49)

A godly husband will bless his wife with his words. He will remember that *love* is a beautiful four-letter word. Sometimes it is best spelled T-I-M-E, and sometimes it is best spelled T-A-L-K.

A Godly Wife Will Bless Her Husband with Her Body (Song 4:1-7)

If a woman is a creature of the ear, a man is a creature of the eye. He is moved by what he sees. Verses 1-7 are a portion of Solomon's song of admiration (it actually goes all the way thru verse 16) as he praises eight different parts of his wife's body. This would continue to bless her with verbal support. Interestingly, he focuses on her upper body. Later, he will praise her from toe to head (7:1-10)! These verses also teach us something about the male and how visual he is when it comes to intimacy. Her body is in full view and Solomon liked, he *loved*, what he saw. Still, he is patient and understanding. What an incredible example he sets for husbands everywhere.

Women in the ancient Near East wore a veil only on special occasions such as the day of their wedding. Solomon says, "Behind your veil, your eyes are doves." The veil both hides and enhances her beauty. His comparing her eyes to doves conveys ideas of peace and purity, tranquility and tenderness, gentleness and innocence (cf. 1:15; 2:14; 5:2). Her eyes speak. They communicate to her husband that she has been calmed and set at rest by his kind and affirming words.

"Your hair is like a flock of goats streaming down Mount Gilead" are words that are strange to our ears, but they would have blessed Shulammite. Viewed from a distance, a herd of black goats streaming or skipping down a mountainside as the sun glistened on their black hair was a beautiful sight. As this wife prepares to give herself to her husband, she lets her hair down. Cascading down her neck and across her shoulders, her beautiful wavy locks excite the sexual desires of her husband. Mount Gilead was a mountain range east of the Jordan River and northeast of the Dead Sea. The region was known for its good and fertile pastures. Shulammite is herself vigorous and fertile on this their wedding night. Letting her hair down signals to Solomon her readiness for him.

Verses 2 and 3 focus on the beauty of her mouth. Her teeth are clean, bright, and white; none are missing! Her "lips are like a scarlet cord" (lit. "thread"). Indeed, her "mouth is lovely." It is beautifully shaped and enticing to her man. There is some question, because of the unusual Hebrew word used here for "mouth," whether Solomon has in view *physical* or *verbal* pleasures that come from her mouth. An either-or decision is unnecessary. "Her mouth is . . . a fertile oasis with lovely words flowing out of it—not to mention possible heavy wet kissing" (Snaith, *Song*, 61). Her lips and her words both are delights of enticement and pleasure.

Her "brow" or temples behind the veil are compared to "a slice of pomegranate." They blushed red with desire and the sweetness of their fruit invites Solomon to kiss them. Pomegranates were considered an aphrodisiac in the ancient world. Attractive to the eye and sweet in flavor, the image appeals to our senses of both sight and taste.

Her neck was "like the tower of David, constructed in layers" with the shields and weapons of Solomon's mighty men (4:4; cf. 3:7-8). She stands tall and graceful. She is neither cowed nor timid. Why should she be in the presence of a man who loves and admires her with such passion and specificity?

Verses 5 and 6 draw attention to Shulammite's breasts. First, they are compared to "two fawns, twins of a gazelle that feed among the lilies."

They are soft and attractive, tender and delicate, making her husband want to touch and caress them gently. Secondly, he describes or names them as two mountains: one he calls the "mountain of myrrh" and the other he calls the "hill of frankincense." Both spices were expensive and used as perfume for the body and the marriage bed. (Proverbs 7:17 informs us that the harlot perfumes her bed with myrrh, aloes, and cinnamon.) The senses of sight and smell are aroused. So enraptured is Solomon that he desires to make love to his wife all night long: "Before the day breaks and the shadows flee."

Time and tenderness are essential twins for a sexually and romantically attractive bedroom. Here we see that slow, romantic foreplay is underway. He praises her specifically and in detail for everything he sees. He gives before receiving. He is as much concerned, if not more so, for her pleasure and satisfaction than he is for his own. He is loving her as Christ has loved us (Eph 5:25ff).

I find it fascinating, at this point, that we really don't know what Shulammite looked like. We have no idea. What we do know is what she looked like to her husband. She was his beauty! In his eyes she was pretty, beautiful, gorgeous; no one compared to her. Indeed, he can say, there is "no imperfection in you" (4:7). This bedroom is going to be a place of unrestrained love: both for our shepherd-king and for his lovely bride.

Express Your Desire for Your Mate
SONG OF SONGS 4:8-11

One can sense the passion that is building in the bedroom as this man lovingly and tenderly prepares his virgin bride for the moment of marital consummation. The two are about to "become one flesh" (Gen 2:24). And like Adam and Eve in the garden of Eden before the fall, "Both the man and his wife were naked, yet felt no shame" (Gen 2:25).

It is also interesting and instructive to see the shift in emphasis from "your" to "my"! The word *my* will appear 20 times in this section, 9 times in 5:1 alone (O'Donnell, *Song*, 80). She is now his and he delights in the gift that she is. She is twice given: both by God and by herself (cf. 8:10-12). He will continue to treat her with honor and respect. He will nourish her and cherish her just as Christ nourishes and cherishes his bride, the church (Eph 5:29).

Invitation: I Want You (Song 4:8)

Solomon's complete attention is on his wife. In biblical intimacy and sex, you will always be focused on your mate before you look to yourself. Then, and only then, is it the right time to take lovemaking to the next level.

The shepherd-king has called his wife his "darling." Now he calls her his "bride," something he will do five times in verses 8-12. He calls her to leave where she is and come to him. Lebanon was near her home. The other mountain ranges mentioned are in the same general area as well. The "dens of the lions and the mountains of the leopards" perhaps represent fears Shulammite may have. Therefore he does not command her; he calls to her. He does not demand; he invites. He invites her to come to him and to leave her fears behind. He will care for her. He will protect her. He will love her. She is his love, his darling. She is his bride, his wife. Sensual anticipation must be clothed with words of safety and security if it expects a warm reception. Solomon's invitation is beautifully delivered.

Captivation: There Is No One Like You (Song 4:9-11)

Solomon tells his bride that she has "captured" or "ravished" his heart (4:9). Her love was so overpowering that he could not resist her. Her love had captured his heart and he could not escape. Just "one glance of her eyes" or seeing "one jewel of her necklace" nearly made his knees buckle. She was enchanting, and he was powerless to resist her spell.

Solomon then says something that again is very strange to our ears. He again calls Shulammite his "bride," but he also refers to her as his "sister," something he will do no less than five times (cf. 4:9-10,12; 5:1-2). We must understand the use of the word in its historical context. In the Ancient Near East *sister* was a term of affection and friendship. In addition to its literal meaning, it could indicate a close and intimate relationship that a husband and wife enjoyed. True lovers will also be true friends, even best friends. This is something Solomon understood well.

Repetition is often a wonderful teacher, and in verse 10 Solomon again calls Shulammite his sister, his bride. He tells her that her love is delightful, and that "it is much better than wine." Wine is intoxicating and sweet, but it could not compare to this. He was drunk with love for her. Charles Spurgeon, the great British preacher of the nineteenth century, said her love was better than wine because it (1) could be enjoyed without question, (2) would never turn sour, (3) would never produce ill effects, and (4) produced a sacred exhilaration (*Most Holy Place*, 13–18).[9]

Her smell also got Solomon's attention. The fragrance or scent of this woman was superior to "any balsam." For a man, sight is closely followed by smell in the sensual realm. Shulammite knew this and so she prepared herself in a way that would draw her man to her, both in sight and smell, and later, in sound (4:16).

Verse 11 moves us into even greater sensual and romantic territory. Her lips, he says, "drip sweetness like the honeycomb," and "honey and milk are under your tongue." The idea that a particular kind of kissing began in France is put to rest by this verse! Deep, wet, sweet, and passionate kissing is at least as old as this Song. Canaan was a land of milk and honey (cf. Exod 3:8). It was a land of promise, joy, blessing, and satisfaction that God graciously provided for the nation of Israel following her enslavement in Egypt. It was a land of sweetness to a people who had been enslaved for more than four hundred years. Solomon found immeasurable joy in the deep, long, and intimate kisses of his bride. He could, as we say today, "just eat her up!"

Besides smelling good herself, she also applied attractive fragrances to her clothes. Lebanon flourished with cedar trees (cf. 1 Kgs 5:6; Pss 29:5; 92:12; 104:16; Isa 2:13; 14:8; Hos 14:5-6). The fresh aroma of those mountain cedars filled the room as the couple made preparation for lovemaking. Virtually all the senses—taste, touch, smell, sight, and sound—have played a role in this sensual symphony in this bedroom. The lovemaking we enjoy will only be enhanced as we follow their example.

Express Your Availability to Your Mate
SONG OF SONGS 4:12-16

One of the greatest gifts a person can give in marriage is exclusive and exciting sex. To enter marriage as a virgin is indeed a precious treasure to bestow on one's spouse. Unfortunately, it is also a rare treasure. The Bible is crystal clear on the issue: any sex outside of marriage is sin in the eyes of God. This includes premarital sex, extra-marital sex, or unnatural sex (such as homosexuality). "Run from sexual immorality" (1 Cor 6:18) is God's command, and a wise person will always listen to God. Shulammite had listened to and obeyed the voice of her God

---

[9] Cited in Paige Patterson, *Song of Solomon* (Chicago: Moody, 1986), 73.

concerning her sexuality. Note the beautiful imagery Solomon uses to describe his virgin bride on their wedding night.

Save Yourself for Your Mate (Song 4:12)

Shulammite is described as "a locked garden" (and possibly "a locked fountain") and "a sealed spring." The imagery pictures her purity and virginity. She had sealed up herself for her husband. She had saved a precious treasure that belonged only to him. I have never known a woman or a man who ever regretted saving sex for marriage. I have, however, known many that regretted not doing so. I think of a letter written to Josh McDowell years ago that probably expresses the regrets of so many scarred by the sexual revolution.

> Dear Mr. McDowell,
>
> Having premarital sex was the most horrifying experience of my life. It wasn't at all the emotionally satisfying experience the world deceived me into believing. I felt as if my insides were being exposed and my heart left unattended. I know God has forgiven me of this haunting sin, but I also know I can never have my virginity back. I dread the day that I have to tell the man I truly love and wish to marry that he is not the only one—though I wish he were. I have stained my life—a stain that will never come out.
>
> Monica[10]

God is pleased, we are protected, and a mate is honored when we keep ourselves pure. Save yourself for marriage. Stay faithful in marriage.

Give Yourself to Your Mate (Song 4:13-15)

Solomon extends the imagery of the garden in verses 13-14, describing his bride as an exotic array of fruits, flowers, plants, trees, and spices. She is paradise regained. She was exceptional and valuable, rare and desirable. She was a fantasy garden, a lover's dream.

> *Your branches are a paradise of pomegranates with choicest fruits,*
> *henna with nard—nard and saffron, calamus and cinnamon, with*
> *all the trees of frankincense, myrrh and aloes, with all the best spices.*

---

[10] Accessed July 9, 2014, http://www.christianliferesources.com/article/helping-your-teen-say-no-to-sex-309.

To find all of this in one garden was unimaginable, and yet in his bride he found them all. She will satisfy his senses of taste, sight, and smell. He will never be bored. He will enjoy the multiple pleasures discovered in this Eden-like garden. Each time would be an exciting time, a new and different adventure. This is redeemed, sanctified sex. The ravaging effects of the fall are reversed!

Solomon now thinks of his wife as "a garden spring, a well of flowing water streaming from Lebanon" (v. 15). To other men she is locked up—enclosed and sealed. For her husband she is wide open—accessible and available. Indeed, her love is overflowing and streaming toward and for him. What she once held back from others she now gives to her husband with unreserved passion and abandonment. Why? Because she had saved herself for this day and this man. She was no casualty of sexual promiscuity. She did not have the wounds of a young 21-year-old who said with pain and sadness in her voice, "I have had 17 partners—too many, I think" (Dalton, "Daughters"). Purity and pleasure go hand in hand when it comes to sex. Again I plead: Save yourself for marriage. It is worth the wait. Give yourself in marriage. You will not be disappointed.

Express Your Satisfaction in Your Mate
SONG OF SONGS 4:16–5:1

Three times in our song we are warned, called to make a solemn vow to "not stir up or awaken love until the appropriate time" (2:7; 3:5; 8:4). The appropriate time has arrived for our shepherd-king and his flawless bride (4:7). For the first time in this particular poem the woman speaks. We have reached the centerpiece, climax, and crescendo of the entire Song. She invites him to make love to her and he is more than ready to oblige! Jack Deere says it well, "She wished to be his with her charms as available as fruit on a tree (cf. 4:13)" ("Song," 1020). She is available and he is ready. The sexual satisfaction on the horizon is a gracious gift from our great Creator God!

There Is Human Satisfaction in Marital Consummation (Song 4:16–5:1)

In beautiful and enticing poetry Shulammite invites Solomon to make love to her. She who has twice said not to "stir up or awaken love until the appropriate time" (cf. 2:7; 3:5) now says, in effect, "The time is right.

I am yours. Come and take me." North winds are strong and south winds more gentle. In lovemaking Shulammite wants and needs both.

She has been listening to every word spoken by her husband, for she picks up on the imagery of the garden of Eden. She is now that garden for him, and her "love" as she calls him is welcome to come in and enjoy. She invites him and she guides him. She tells him what she is feeling and what she wants. Great sex is the result of good communication. All the physical parts fit when a man and woman come together, but sex is no mere mechanical union. It is a personal and spiritual union nurtured by careful communication. We cannot be certain of all that is meant by the imagery of coming to the garden and tasting the choice fruits, but it is not difficult to imagine all sorts of good things that this couple will share!

The first verse of chapter 5 records the aftermath of their sexual consummation. The couple has made love. They were not disappointed. They had planned for it, saved themselves for it, studied up on it, and talked about it. All of their time and effort has been rewarded.

Shulammite invited Solomon to come to "his garden" in 4:16. Now in 5:1 he calls her "my" garden. In fact, nine times in this one verse he uses the word *my*. In tender words he calls Shulammite his garden, his sister, and his bride. Coming in to her was indeed a garden of delight. She smelled good, tasted good, and felt good; and he told her so. Their lovemaking was delightful. It had been wonderful. She invited him to come to her and he did. In response, he romantically and tenderly expressed the pleasure she had given him.

There Is Divine Satisfaction in Marital Consummation (Song 5:1)

The last part of verse 1 has created quite a bit of interpretive discussion. Exactly who is it that encourages this man and woman in their lovemaking? Some believe it is the friends of the couple. The HCSB identifies the speaker as the book's narrator. However, this speaker's intimate knowledge of all that has transpired in their bedroom leads me in a different direction.

Though His name never appears directly in the entire Song of Songs (but see 2:7; 3:5; 8:4,6), I believe the one who speaks here is God. He is the unseen but present guest in their bedroom. He has observed all that has happened this night, and He tells us what He thinks about it. And He thinks it is a good thing!

"Eat, friends! Drink, be intoxicated with love!" The love shared by Solomon and Shulammite, together with the gift of sex, was given to them by God. Craig Glickman comments,

> He [God] lifts His voice and gives hearty approval to the entire night. He vigorously endorses and affirms the love of this couple. He takes pleasure in what has taken place. He is glad they have drunk deeply of the fountain of love. Two of His own have experienced love in all the beauty and fervor and purity that He intended for them. In fact, He urges them on to more. . . . That is His attitude toward the giving of their love to each other. And by the way, that's also His attitude toward couples today. (Glickman, *Song*, 25)

Yes, God is there and He is pleased with what He sees. "He sees the passion. He hears the sighs of delight. He watches the lovers as they caress one another in the most intimate places. He is witness to the fleshly, earthly sights, sounds, and smells. . . . God desires for us to rejoice in our sensuousness, to give in to it" (Dillow and Pintus, *Intimate*, 17).

A term of tender affection flows from the mouth of God in this verse as He looks on the couple enjoying His good gift of sex as He designed it. He calls them "friends." God loves them, and He loves what He sees. How foreign this is to so many persons' thinking when they try to imagine what God the Creator thinks about sex. He loves us, and He likes it when we are engaged in the passion of lovemaking within the covenant of marriage. It can be revolutionary and transforming when we accurately and correctly understand the Creator's perspective. We can become like a woman named Beth who said,

> Loving my husband can become an act of worship to God. As my husband and I lie together, satiated in the afterglow of sexual ecstasy, the most natural thing in the world is for me to offer thanksgiving to my God for the beauty, the glory of our sexual joy. I don't even think about what I am doing; my heart just turns to the Lord and offers praise. Truly His gift of sex is a wondrous thing. (Dillow and Pintus, *Intimate*, 19)

Practical Applications from Song of Songs 4:1–5:1

What do happy couples say about sex, this good gift from a great God? *Reader's Digest* ran an article that answers that question with the caption,

"With a dash of surprise, a pinch of romance and a word or two at the right moment, love can be kept simmering even in the longest marriage." Adapting their list slightly, I think at least 12 things can be said. Any couple will be well served to meditate, reflect on, and put into practice these helpful ideas.

What Happy Couples Say about Sex

1. They make sex a priority; it is important to them.
2. They make time for sex.
3. They stay emotionally intimate.
4. They know how to touch and what works.
5. They keep romance alive by meeting each other's needs.
6. They keep their sexual anticipation alive.
7. They know how to play and foreplay (both in and out of bed).
8. They know how to talk to each other.
9. They remain lovers and friends.
10. They maintain a sense of humor and know how to laugh.
11. They want to please each other.
12. They cherish each other as a sacred and precious gift of God. ("What Happy Couples Say," 13–16).

How Does This Text Exalt Christ?

The King's Beautiful Bride

In our Song we see a bride whose husband views her as perfect, flawless, "with no imperfection" (4:7). If only such a bride really existed. The fact is, however, she does! She exists in the people of God called the church, a people God has redeemed and "purchased with His own blood" (Acts 20:28). Made new in Jesus Christ, her divine Bridegroom, she knows He is committed "to make her holy, cleansing her with the washing of water by the word," and that He is doing this "to present the church to Himself in splendor, without spot or wrinkle or anything like that, but holy and blameless" (Eph 5:26-27).

This is how our Bridegroom sees us through His imputed righteousness, and this is who we are predestined to be when our marriage is consummated at "the marriage feast of the Lamb" (Rev 19:9; cf. Rom 8:30). On that day we will *be glad, rejoice, and give Him glory, because the marriage of the Lamb has come, and His wife has prepared herself. She [will be] given fine linen to wear, bright and pure. For the fine linen represents the righteous acts of the saints.* (Rev 19:7-8)

The love this shepherd-king has for his bride is beautiful and precious indeed. However, as Robert Saucy says so well,

The love of Christ for His bride far surpasses anything known in the human level. . . . Never has a husband loved as Christ loved the church. For Christ did not love those worthy of love, but sinners and enemies (Rom 5:8-10). . . . "Christ loved the church not because it was perfectly lovable but in order to make it such." (Saucy, *The Church*, 45)[11]

Indeed the extent of His love is seen in the price He paid to make us flawless, with no imperfection at all. We are indeed His beautiful bride, His darling. This is how Christ sees us! This is what He has made us!

"The Bride of Christ"

O Church of God, thou spotless bride,
On Jesus' breast secure;
No stains of sin in thee abide
Thy garments all are pure.
Of unity and holiness
Thy gentle voice doth sing;
Of purity and lowliness
Thy songs in triumph ring.

Thou lovely virgin, thou are fair,
Thy mother's only child;
Thy heav'nly music let me hear,
Thy voice is sweet and mild.
Thy cheeks adorned with jewels bright,
Thy neck with chains of gold;
Unfurl thy banners in thy might,
Thy graces rich unfold.

---

[11] The last portion of this quote comes from Brooke Foss Westcott, *Saint Paul's Epistle to the Ephesians* (Grand Rapids, MI: Eerdmans, 1952), 84.

She stood attired in spotless dress
The early morning through,
And then into the wilderness
On eagle's wings she flew.
And nourished there from heav'nly clime,
She lived for many years;
Now, in this blessed evening time
Her glory reappears.

She leans upon an Arm of Love
No sin her garments taints;
They're made of linen wov'n above—
The righteousness of saints.
The marriage of the Lamb is come,
His bride all ready stands;
The Bridegroom soon will take her home
To dwell in heav'nly lands.
　　　(Brooks and Byers, "The Bride of Christ," public domain)

Reflect and Discuss

1. Why should God be glorified when married couples engage in sex? Do couples need to do anything special to glorify God in sex?
2. Discuss the ways sexual activity (or lack thereof) might affect our lives as Christians. How have you seen these in your marriage?
3. Why is the brain one of the most important sexual organs? How can a husband love his wife through her heart and mind?
4. Why must biblical intimacy and sex always be focused on one's mate before it looks to self?
5. Solomon calls Shulammite his sister. What does this mean, and what can we learn from his words and feelings?
6. Why is sex reserved in a biblical worldview for a man and a woman who are married? How does this connect to the gospel?
7. Why should a husband and wife make themselves available to one another? How can they communicate this?
8. What does it mean for God to be the "unseen guest" of the bedroom? Why can couples rejoice in this fact?
9. How does the purity of this bride prefigure the consummation of all things when Jesus returns for His bride, the Church?
10. How does the love Solomon has for Shulammite prefigure the work of Jesus on our behalf?

What Do You Do When the Honeymoon Comes to an End?

SONG OF SONGS 5:2-8

Main Idea: Because of sin, all marriages will experience hardship. Because of the gospel, biblical marriages will be filled with persistent love, radical grace, true repentance, and joyful reconciliation.

I.   Anticipate the Challenges of Time (5:2).
II. Beware of the Sin of Selfishness (5:3).
III. Expect Seasons of Regret (5:4-6).
IV. Receive the Blows that Lead to Repentance (5:7).
V.   Pursue the Joys of Reconciliation (5:8).

Honeymoons are wonderful times of excitement, fun, happiness, joy, and love. We get married like Solomon and Shulammite in Song of Songs 3:6-11, bask in the passion of our wedding night (4:1–5:1), and think this is the way that it is always going to be. But then we return home to the real world with all of its demands and responsibilities, and before long the glow of the honeymoon has faded into a flicker of a lackluster routine. Disappointment sets in. Expectations are not met. Questions begin to haunt us: Is this what I signed up for? Is this what I am going to endure for the rest of my life? Did I make a mistake in marrying this person?

If you have found yourself asking these kinds of questions, I have some good news for you. Everyone has! Every couple in their marriage is going to have peaks and valleys, good days and bad days, good weeks and bad weeks, and I can expand the calendar if you like! And those bad times can often make their way into the bedroom. For many years, when I speak on the subject of marriage, I have repeatedly said to the couples present, "What takes place outside the bedroom will influence what takes place inside the bedroom."

In our text our couple has married and celebrated their wedding by sexually consummating their union. Commentators universally point out that Song of Songs 5:1 "lies at the center of the Song. This is true in word count, in the order of events and in tone and intensity" (Griffiths,

Song, 114). However, in 5:2 we return to real life and immediately we find our couple experiencing trouble. There are problems already in paradise. Paul Griffiths succulently says, "After the orgasmic culmination of 5:1, voice, place, and tone shift suddenly" (*Song*, 117). However, with this shift comes some very helpful and practical wisdom for all as we adjust in marriage, work through conflict, and emerge on the other side reconciled and reunited. The honesty of the Bible is so refreshing. We are all going to experience times of difficulty. Marriage involves two depraved human beings trying to figure out how to get along. Again the good news is that we can, and Scripture is a helpful guide in getting us where God wants us to be.

Anticipate the Challenges of Time
SONG OF SONGS 5:2

Our text again presents a bedroom scene, most likely a dream and a time of separation (cf. 3:1-4). Previously this took place while they were courting. Now they are married. Times of separation would disappear or at least be kept to a minimum. At least that is what Shulammite thought. However, things have not worked out as she had hoped. She is alone in bed (again?!), dreaming, and tossing and turning. Where is he? Why is he late again? Why does it seem like he thinks spending time with others is more important than spending time with me? I know he is the king, but I am his wife. *Love* is a beautiful four-letter word, and for me it is best spelled T-I-M-E.

Suddenly she is awakened. "A sound! My love is knocking!" Note that our text records his saying at the end of the verse: "For my head is drenched with dew, my hair with droplets of the night." This is an example of Hebrew parallelism and indicates that he has arrived home late. It is probably near or even after midnight. No doubt he had had a long, hard day, and his day had run into night. On this particular occasion *work* won out over the *wife* and the challenge of time management had beaten them. The stage is perfectly set for a confrontation, a showdown in the bedroom.

Solomon may have anticipated there might be a problem, some potential for a fight. A locked bedroom door would be a big hint! His approach is commendable: gentle and sensitive. It's not going to work, but give him credit for trying! He speaks to his wife using four terms of affection, each preceded by the personal possessive pronoun *my*. We have seen these tender descriptions before. Perhaps he thought, "They worked before; maybe they will work now."

My sister (cf. 4:8). You are my friend as well as my lover. I have a familial love and affection for you.

My darling (cf. 1:9; used 9 times in the Song). Some translate it "my love." I delight in you. I take pleasure in you. You have my heart.

My dove (2:14). This may be a pet name. You are gentle and pure. I find peace and tranquility in your presence.

My perfect one (4:7). You are flawless and blameless. It is instructive to note that this is the goal for which Jesus Christ redeems His bride (Eph 5:26-27).

Solomon is working hard to redeem the evening, but unfortunately we are headed for a bad night, a disappointing night, in the bedroom. Bob Turnbull, in an article entitled "What Your Wife Really Wants," reminds us that wives can dry up and wither on the inside if four things are missing in our marriage:

Time. The currency of a relationship; clearing space in your calendar for her says, "You are valuable to me."

Talk. This is how she connects with you. It is also a way she handles stress. Men, on the other hand, often take flight in response to stress (Peterson, "To Fight Stress").

Tenderness. It feeds her soul when she is nourished and knows she is cherished.

Touch. Non-sexual, affectionate touch is crucial to a wife. And if she only receives it as the pre-game warm-up to sex, she will begin to feel used, like a marital prostitute. (List adapted from Turnbull and Turnbull, "What Your Wife Really Wants")

Beware of the Sin of Selfishness
SONG OF SONGS 5:3

Few sins are more lethal in marriage than the sin of selfishness. At its root, it is a form of idolatry. In our text it is clear that the husband disappointed his wife and let her down. He failed the "4-T" test we just noted. However, this does not justify the response of Shulammite. Basically, her response says, "I don't have time for you. Serving you would be too much trouble." Note the following phrases:

"I have taken off my clothing. How can I put it back on?" It is too much trouble to put on my robe. And think what you are missing beneath these sheets because you were out late.

"I have washed my feet. How can I get them dirty?" I am bathed, clean, and in bed. It's time to go to sleep.

Her two-fold objection in our modern vernacular would translate, "Not tonight; I'm tired." "Not tonight; I have a headache." "Getting up would give me a headache." "Not tonight; I'm not in the mood." You came home late. You didn't even call. I will deny you. I will punish you. Knock all you want; that door is staying locked!

Let's get practical and honest at this point. All couples fight. Every couple will experience conflict and disagreements. The issue is not *whether* we will fight, but *how* we will fight. Will we fight dirty or will we fight fair? I am not sure where I found it, but I have personally benefited from a short article entitled "Ten Tips on Fighting Fair." Solomon and Shulammite certainly would have been helped by it. And take special note how the ten items focus more on the other person than they do on you. Selfishness and self-centeredness are almost completely absent from these words of wisdom.

Ten Tips on Fighting Fair

1. **Confront problems** as soon as possible after they arise. Don't allow them to fester and cause bitterness.
2. **Master the art of listening**. Show your mate respect by hearing her or him out. Ask for clarification if you don't understand. Be patient. Don't hurry the conversation.
3. **Limit the discussion** of the conflict to the present issue. Don't drag out yesterday's (or last year's!) dirty laundry. Being "historical" will infect the conversation.
4. **Use "I" messages** in making your point and expressing your emotions. This allows you to take responsibility for your feelings, and it also allows the other person to hear about your feelings without feeling defensive. "You" messages tend to be perceived as attacks and criticism. Why? Because they are!
5. **Avoid exaggerations** such as "always," "never," etc. Such statements are seldom true simply because as inconsistent human beings we very seldom "always" or "never" do anything.

6. **Avoid character assassination** (name calling and putdowns). Pointing out character flaws or demeaning another person will do nothing but stir up greater disharmony.

7. **Use appropriate words and actions** for the matter at hand. Not all arguments are worth fighting at peak volume. The fact is, no argument is worth fighting at peak volume.

8. **Don't be concerned about winning or losing** the argument. It's better if both parties can be more concerned about resolving the conflict rather than who "wins" or "loses." *Compromise* is a good word and a valuable goal in this context.

9. **Determine limits.** Comments that are hurtful or damaging must be avoided. Speak to your mate in the way you want your mate to speak to you.

10. **Choose to forgive.** All people fail. If we don't give others a chance to start over after failure, our relationships will suffer. Complete forgiveness may take time, depending on the degree of hurt caused by the other person. However, it's important to have an attitude of forgiveness and to keep asking God to help you get to the point where you can truly forgive. Remembering how much you have been forgiven by Christ is essential at this point (Eph 4:32).

Expect Seasons of Regret
SONG OF SONGS 5:4-6

Have you ever had the experience of thinking, "I sure wish I had not said that"? Or maybe you've thought, "I sure wish I hadn't done that." I suspect we all have. At least I hope you have because we all make mistakes in marriage. We all do things that sooner or later we regret. This was certainly true for Shulammite. First, she locked the door to their bedroom. Second, she told her husband to take a hike! He was not worth the trouble of getting out of bed and putting her robe back on. His sweet talk in verse 2 would not work this time. As anyone would know, this would have been devastating to the all-too-fragile male ego.

However, this man is different. He does not give up, at least not yet. Shulammite tells us in verse 4, "My love thrust his hand through the opening, and my feelings were stirred for him." Six times in 5:2-8 Shulammite calls her husband "my love." She will do so four more times in verses 9-10. Solomon makes one final attempt to win her heart. He gently "thrust his hand through the opening." Because our Song is poetic, symbolic, and erotic, many scholars believe we have a double entendre at work. Several times in Scripture the male hand is used euphemistically for the sexual part of a man (see Isa 57:8,10; "authority" in Jer 5:31). That would also mean the word translated "opening" corresponds to the female's sexual parts. Shulammite's response would seem to support this understanding. She says, "My feelings were stirred for him." The ESV says, "My heart was thrilled within me." The NIV: "My heart began to pound for him." Whatever harsh feelings she had were being vanquished by his kind words and persistent pursuit.

Verse 5 says, "I rose to open for my love. My hands dripped with myrrh, my fingers with flowing myrrh on the handles of the bolt." The "I" is emphatic in the Hebrew text. She jumps out of bed, apparently not taking time to clothe herself, quickly perfumes herself (though the text could mean that Solomon left the myrrh on the handle as a token of love), and hurries to the door now ready for a time of intimacy and lovemaking. Time to make up!

Unfortunately, it is too late. Verse 6 notes, "I opened to my love, but my love had turned and gone away. I was crushed that he had left. I sought him, but did not find him. I called him, but he did not answer." Wounded males often go into shells. They just walk away. One can hear the heartbroken regret in Shulammite's words. He's gone. I'm crushed. I can't find him. He's not answering (or taking my calls). This has not worked out at all like I hoped or expected.

If Solomon earlier failed the "4-T" test, perhaps Shulammite failed the "4-C" test. Yvonne Turnbull, in "What Your Husband Really Wants," notes four things a husband longs to receive from his wife. Ladies, this is who he wants you to be:

His cheerleader. A man thrives on his wife's approval and praise.

His champion. A wife's respect and encouragement lifts a man's spirit and his sense of self-worth.

His companion. A man wants his wife to be his best friend.

His complement. A woman is necessary to complete a man. (Adapted from Turnbull and Turnbull, "What Your Husband Really Wants")

A single friend of mine playfully says, "Being single makes for lonely nights but it sure makes for peaceful days." A married man longs for both peaceful days and intimate nights. Where those things are absent, regret is certain to follow.

Receive the Blows that Lead to Repentance
SONG OF SONGS 5:7

In 2 Corinthians 7:9-10 Paul writes,

> *Now I rejoice, not because you were grieved, but because your grief led to repentance. For you were grieved as God willed, so that you didn't experience any loss from us. For godly grief produces a repentance not to be regretted and leading to salvation, but worldly grief produces death.*

Because of the content and nature of Song of Songs 5:7, I am all the more convinced this section of our Song is a dream. It is virtually impossible to believe Solomon's wife, the queen of Israel, would be treated the way she seems to be treated in this verse. First, "The guards who go about the city found me." She cannot find her husband but she is found by the police who guard the streets and walls of the city. She is seeking her man (v. 6) but only runs into other men, men she views as little more than a desert (1:14)! Second, "They beat and wound me." Third, "They took my cloak" (or veil). She is stopped, struck, and stripped. Though interpretive certainty is not possible, I see here the blows of repentance given to her by the Lord that will lead to restoration and reconciliation with her husband. Dennis Kinlaw raises the questions, "Does this treatment by the watchmen reflect the girl's guilt and sense of failure at the slowness of her response to her husband?" ("Song," 1232). I believe it does. Griffiths refers to it as "a love wound" (*Song*, 125). Having been broken—heartbroken—she now acts on her change of heart. It is painful. It hurts. In her case, it is even humiliating. However, it is worth it.

In another book of wisdom, the book of Job, we find words that closely parallel the words of this verse. There, in Job 23:8-10, we read,

> *If I go east, He is not here, and if I go west, I cannot perceive Him. When He is at work to the north, I cannot see Him; when He turns south, I cannot find Him. Yet He knows the way I have taken; when He has tested me, I will emerge as pure gold.*

Charles Spurgeon said of repentance, "It is a discovery of the evil of sin, a mourning that we have committed it, a resolution to forsake it. It is, in fact, a change of mind of a very deep and practical character" ("Apostolic Exhortation"). This is beautifully put on display by Shulammite in this verse. Her wounds went deep, but her healing would be complete.

Pursue the Joys of Reconciliation
SONG OF SONGS 5:8

The full fruit of Shulammite's reconciliation with Solomon is beautifully detailed in 5:9ff. However, its seed is deposited for us to see here in 5:8. Once again Shulammite calls to her girlfriends, "the young women of Jerusalem." Shulammite has previously charged them in 2:7 and 3:5. She will do so again in 8:5 with the same exact oath. Here her charge is different. Regret led to repentance, which now leads to a longing for reconciliation. What Shulammite is about to say is important, and she wants there to be witnesses to her words. Further, she, in essence, calls on her girlfriends to join in her reconnaissance mission. My friend Bill Cutrer, who is now in heaven, said, "Shulammite sends a message of her present, repentant, anxious desires for her lover" ("Unpublished Notes").

What is her charge? Listen to it in several translations:

If you find my love, tell him I am lovesick. (HCSB)

If you find my beloved, what will you tell him? Tell him I am faint with love. (NIV 1984)

If you find my beloved . . . tell him I am sick with love. (ESV)

If you find my lover, please tell him I want him, that I'm heartsick with love for him. (MSG)

Our bride loves her man and she wants everyone to know it—especially him. She is weighed down with lovesickness for him, a strong and powerful image. She grieves over his absence and separation, and she will not stand for it. She is looking for him and she enlists others to join her in the search. Whoever finds him first is to let him know that she loves him, she desires him, she wants him. What kind of man is her man that she would speak so boldly and publicly? The answer will follow in 5:10-16. No wonder she longed to be reconciled to her man. No wonder he wanted the same thing, too (6:4-10).

In marriage, the eye finds, the heart chooses, the hand binds, and only death should loose. Howard Markman said while speaking at Duquesne University in October 1999, "It's not how much you love each other, but when conflicts arise, [it's] how you handle them that determines the success of your marriage or relationship." George Worgul of Duquesne University also added, "Many people want to have good relationships and enjoy a happy marriage. Love, however, is hard work" (cited in Akin, *God on Sex*, 177–78). Both men were right. Marriage is hard work. But it is worthwhile work, and when the work is pursued following *God's guidelines* and seeking *His glory*, you'll enjoy a Christian marriage and discover a Christian bedroom as our great God intended: one that is satisfying, liberated, sensual, erotic, intimate, and pleasing both to God and one another. With a commitment to Jesus and to one another, and the courage to stay with it no matter what, we can find the joy God planned for all of us. On the other side of repentance, reconciliation is waiting.

Practical Applications from Song of Songs 5:2-8

Relationships are a challenge in a fallen world ravaged by sin. This is especially true when it comes to marriage. Two sinners saved by the grace of God through faith in Jesus Christ are still sinners. They need the enablement of His Spirit and the instruction of His Word to be a blessing rather than a curse to their mates. Simply put, they need His attitude; they need His mind (Phil 2:5). Below are ten principles that "flesh out" the mind of Christ to help us restore, redeem, and rejoice in the relationships of life. They are exactly the things our shepherd-king and his beautiful bride needed to get their marriage back on track.

How to Bless Rather Than Curse Your Relationships

1. Make a choice (commitment) to accept your mate, recognizing that she or he was made in God's image (Gen 1:26-27) and that Christ died for your mate (John 3:16). Accepting people does not entail always affirming their actions (Phil 2:3-5).
2. Receive your mate as someone valuable in your life. God will use him or her to conform you more to the image of His Son (Rom 8:28-30).
3. Accept personal responsibility for your relationship. Do not play the blame game (Prov 14:16; 15:12,32; 28:13; Eph 4:29-31).
4. Rejoice in and value your differences, looking for the positive.
5. Determine to communicate in a godly manner (Prov 4:24; 10:11,19-21,31-32; 26:20-28) by:
   - sharing (Prov 11:13-14; 25:11-12; Eph 4:15),
   - listening (Prov 12:15; 15:22; 19:27; 21:23; 29:11,20; Jas 1:19), and
   - talking (Prov 15:1,23,28; 16:24; Eph 4:25-27).

6. Never assume anything. Grow in your understanding of your mate (Prov 3:3-4,7; 17:27-28; 18:1-2,13,15; 19:2).
7. Be an encourager (Prov 3:27; 12:25; 15:15; 17:22; 1 Cor 8:1; 13:7).
8. Be real: be honest and willing to admit your own failures. Learn to say, "I am sorry; I was wrong. Will you forgive me?" (Eph 4:32; Jas 5:16).
9. Accept yourself *in Christ* (Gal 2:20; Eph 1:3-14). It will free you to love and accept others without either a superiority or inferiority complex (1 Cor 13:4).
10. Be a *lover*: learn to speak in a language that your mate will understand (1 Cor 13:4-8). Remember Gary Chapman's wisdom of the 5 love languages:
    *   Words
    *   Touch
    *   Service
    *   Gifts
    *   Time

How Does This Text Exalt Christ?

See the King Who Pursues His Bride

A Hebrew person reading this text would have been surprised, if not stunned, by the rebuff of Shulammite to Solomon her king. They would also be amazed at his gentle pleading and request. Kings don't plead; they demand. Kings don't beg; they command. At least that is true of most earthly kings. By contrast, this shepherd-king, this lover, stands at the door knocking, asking his bride to let him enter that they might enjoy sweet communion and intimacy. Would the world ever see such a king with such power and grace all wrapped up in one man? Yes it would!

In Revelation 3:20 we see "the Alpha and the Omega" (Rev 1:8), "the First and the Last" (Rev 1:17), "the Amen, the faithful and true Witness" (Rev 3:14), the "KING OF KINGS AND LORD OF LORDS" (Rev 19:16) standing at the door of His church gently knocking. What are the tender and pleading words that flow from His mouth? "Listen! I stand at the door and knock. If anyone hears My voice and opens the door, I will come in to him and have dinner with him, and he with Me" (Rev 3:20). That precious invitation from the great King is for you! It is for me! It is an invitation to be restored to a right relationship with your Creator (Rev 3:14). It is an invitation to be reconciled with your

Shepherd-King who has redeemed you by His blood (Rev 5:9). One greater than Solomon desires to enter into sweet, spiritual intimacy with His chosen ones. He stands at the door gently knocking. If I might paraphrase an old gospel hymn written in 1880 by Will Thompson,

> Softly and tenderly Jesus is calling,
> Calling for you and for me,
> Here, at the door, He's waiting and knocking,
> Watching for you and for me.
> Why should we tarry when Jesus is pleading,
> Pleading for you and for me?
> Why should we linger and heed not His mercies,
> Mercies for you and for me?
> Oh, for the wonderful love He has promised,
> Promised for you and for me!
> Though we have sinned, He has mercy and pardon,
> Pardon for you and for me. (Thompson, "Softly and Tenderly")

Reflect and Discuss

1. Why will all marriages experience times of difficulty? Why is it so important to keep this truth in mind throughout a marriage?
2. How can the challenges of time put a strain on a marriage? What are some practical ways you can prepare and guard against this strain?
3. How is selfishness a form of idolatry? In what areas are you most selfish?
4. What are some ways couples fight, like Shulammite, unfairly? How can the "Ten Tips" in this chapter help address these tendencies?
5. Why can we expect to have regrets in marriage? How does the gospel relate to our regrets?
6. Explain the complexities of verse 7. How does this verse fit into the story of Solomon and Shulammite?
7. Why is repentance so painful? What other passages in Scripture speak to repentance in the believer's life?
8. In what ways have you experienced marriage as hard work? Does reconciliation make the work worth it?
9. How can you be a blessing rather than a curse to your mate?
10. Share your story about how Jesus called after you with His soft and persistent knocking. How can you show this same love toward your mate?

The Marks of a Redeemed and Reconciled Relationship

SONG OF SONGS 5:9–6:10

Main Idea: In a marriage that reflects Christ's redeeming love, a husband and wife will each work to serve one another in order to overcome the troubles that will inevitably come.

I. **The Woman Has Her Part to Do (5:9–6:3).**
   A. There are things you should say (5:9-16).
      1. Praise his uniqueness (5:10).
      2. Note his attractiveness (5:11-16).
      3. Cultivate his friendship (5:16).
   B. There are things you should do (6:1-3).
      1. Study his tendencies (6:1-2).
      2. Welcome his advances (6:3).
II. **The Man Has His Part to Do (6:4-10).**
   A. Tell her she is beautiful (6:4).
   B. Tell her she is irresistible (6:5-7).
   C. Tell her she is special (6:8-9).
   D. Tell her she is awesome (6:10).

Years ago a singing group called "The Stylistics" sang a song that burrows down to the soul. It was entitled "Break Up to Make Up." Unfortunately, the song captures the experience of far too many couples. They find themselves in a never-ending cycle of breaking up and making up, hating and loving, fighting and reconciling. But it does not have to be this way. We must never forget the insight of J. C. Ryle: "Marriage is, after all, the union of two sinners, and not two angels" (*Expository Thoughts*, 200). But in Christ we are two sinners saved by grace and empowered by the Holy Spirit. We are new creatures in Christ (2 Cor 5:17) who are supernaturally enabled to navigate the challenges of married life and emerge better, reconciled, and moving forward on the other side. Elisabeth Elliot is spot on when she says, "When sinful people live in the same world, and especially when they work in the same office and sleep in the same bed, they sin against each other. Troubles

141

arise. Some of those troubles are very serious and not subject to easy solutions." The good news? She notes, "God knows all about them, and knew about them long before they happened. He made provision for them" (Elliot, *Trusting God*, 96).

Our God has indeed made provision in Christ, and in this portion of the Song of Songs He also provides wisdom that will lead to reconciliation, and that will help us bear the marks of a redeemed relationship, a relationship nurtured and nourished by the gospel of Jesus Christ.

The Woman Has Her Part to Do
SONG OF SONGS 5:9–6:3

In our Song, the happy couple hit a bump in the road in 5:2-8. There was some bad timing, hurt feelings, and an unhappy night in the bedroom. However, this couple loves each other and will not allow their relationship to stay sidetracked. They will put in the hard work necessary to work through their problems. The honeymoon may be over, but their marriage is just beginning. They are in for the long haul, and they will work to make it work.

In marriage both the woman and the man have roles and responsibilities. As those redeemed by Christ, we are not takers but givers. Our focus is not on ourselves but the other person. In our Song, Shulammite is determined to do her part and to do it well. Her God should be honored. Her husband should be blessed.

There Are Things She Should Say (Song 5:9-16)

Given her expression of love for her man in verse 8, Shulammite is challenged in verse 9. You say you are "lovesick" over this guy? Then tell us why. Twice they ask, "What makes him better than another?" Further, you charged us, you put us under oath. This is serious. So help us understand. What is so special about your love that he arouses the feelings of illness or fainting (Hess, *Song*, 179)?

Shulammite welcomes the challenge. In fact, it is almost like she invites it. Yes, I am lovesick over this man and you would be too if you knew what a man, what a mighty fine man he is. So let me tell you. What follows is real good!

Praise his uniqueness (5:10). Shulammite admires and respects her husband and showers him with a catalog of praise in verses 10-16. She begins by calling him "my love" and pointing out how exceptional he is. Yes, he is "fit and strong" ("radiant and ruddy," ESV, HCSB margin). Glickman translates it "dazzlingly ruddy" (*Song*, 66). But better and more important than that, he is "notable among ten thousand." There is no man like my man, at least in my eyes. He stands out from and above all the rest. One can only imagine how this would make her husband feel.

Note his attractiveness (5:11-16). Shulammite begins to describe the physical attractiveness of her husband, though issues of character are implied as well. This is the only physical description of the man in the Song. In contrast, there are three of the woman (4:1-7; 6:4-10; 7:1-9).

"His head is purest gold" indicating great wealth and value in her eyes. "His hair is wavy and black as a raven," perhaps a reference to his youthful vitality. "He is neither gray nor bald" (Garrett, *Proverbs*, 414).

In verse 12 she says, "His eyes are like doves beside streams of water, washed in milk and set like jewels." Looking into her love's eyes she sees peace, gentleness, calmness, and tranquility, brightness and alertness. Like his hair, they are attractive to her.

Verse 13 informs us that his cologne radiates a sweet smell like "beds of spices." And his lips? They are lilies "dripping with flowing myrrh." They are sweet, offering the wet, passionate kisses she longs to receive. He has aroused her sense of sight, smell, and taste.

Verses 14-15 address particular parts of his body. His arms are strong and valuable, like "rods of gold set within topaz." His body is "an ivory panel covered with sapphires." He is handsome, carved and cut, powerful and strong. His body "possesses the might necessary to carry the rest of his muscular frame and to protect the female from harm, such as the beating the guards inflicted upon her (5:7)" (Hess, *Song*, 185). His legs are also strong and sturdy, like "alabaster pillars set on pedestals of pure gold." Indeed his appearance is breathtaking, almost statuesque. He conjures up images of the majestic cedars of Lebanon.

In verse 16 she returns to his face, specifically his mouth. It is nothing less than pure sweetness. And he is nothing less than "absolutely desirable." This strong masculine male is her hero, her champion. He is the man with whom she has chosen to share and spend her life, and she has no regrets. This is my love, ladies of Jerusalem. In my eyes no one comes close in comparison. But there's more.

Cultivate his friendship (5:16). Shulammite tells the young women of Jerusalem that her husband, "my love," is also "my friend." There is tremendous significance in this statement. Whenever I do premarital counseling, I always ask the couple before me if they like each other.

Not, Do you *love* each other? But, Do you *like* each other? I then challenge them, as strongly as I know how, to work at becoming one another's best friend. I then tell them if they do, I can make two promises to
them. First, their marriage will be a blessing because it is a blessing to
hang out with your best friend. Second, their marriage will go the distance because best friends do not give up on their best friends.

A husband and wife should be lovers. They should also be best
friends. By God's grace I have found both in my wife Charlotte. And as
we grow old together, our friendship grows more and more precious
with each passing year. Proverbs 18:24 says, "There is a friend who stays
closer than a brother." A husband longs for that friend to be his wife.

There Are Things You Should Do (Song 6:1-3)

Throughout the Song of Songs we see the importance of balancing what
we say with what we do. Both are important in building a healthy relationship. Our bride has said some wonderful things about her man in
5:10-16. She will now complement those statements with her actions.
Her acts are subtle, but they still speak loud and clear.

Study his tendencies (6:1-2). The young women of Jerusalem have
another question for Shulammite (cf. 5:9). They actually ask two. You
have told us *why* you love him. Now we want to know *where* he is! "Where
has your love gone most beautiful of women?" (cf. 1:8; 5:9). "Which way
has he turned? We will seek him with you." We will be glad to help you
if you don't know.

Well the fact is she does know where he is because she knows
her man. She knows what he likes and where he likes to go. She has
become a student of her husband, and in her study she has grown in her
knowledge and understanding of Solomon. In verse 2 "she uses sexually charged language and essentially says, 'He is with me'" (Garrett,
Proverbs, 415). She informs the young women of Jerusalem, "My love has
gone down to his garden," he has come back to me (4:16–5:1). He loves
me and loves loving me. He is enjoying "the beds of spices," perhaps a
hint at multiple enjoyments of lovemaking. Further, he is right at home
when he is with me. He is "feeding in the gardens and gathering lilies."
He is enjoying my body and our lovemaking. We are kissing (see lips as
lilies in 5:13) and we are engaging in the joyful intimacies of marriage
(see 2:16).

Welcome his advances (6:3). Once more we have returned to Eden
before the fall. They are in the garden together, naked and with no

shame (Gen 2:25). Shulammite gladly welcomes and receives the advances of her love. As she boldly proclaims, "I am my love's and my love is mine; he feeds among the lilies." I foolishly refused his advances earlier in this dream, this nightmare (5:2-3), but not now. I belong to him and he belongs to me. He is welcome in my garden. I want him there, and I want him to know it.

This wife says to her husband, "I am available to you. I am here for your enjoyment. And I desire you too. I want you too. Our bedroom is again a garden of delight. I know sex is important to you, and because it is important to you, it is important to me."

Sex is important to a healthy and vibrant marriage. Phil McGraw, author of *Relationship Rescue*, says, "If you have a good sexual relationship, it's about 10% of the value of the relationship overall. If you don't have a good sexual relationship, it's about 90%" (Goodnow, "Phil McGraw").

The Man Has His Part to Do
SONG OF SONGS 6:4-10

This woman has done her part to reconcile with her husband after a marital spat one night. I would say she went the extra mile and then some. Now it is the man's turn to respond and do his part. He does not let his wife down. As a man of God whose poetic description in 5:10-16 points us to the vision of Christ in Revelation 1:13-16(!), he wants to love his wife well. He wants to provide for her and care for her as our Lord does His bride (Eph 5:29).

Solomon knows the way to her heart is through her ears, and so once more he speaks to her with words of love and affection (cf. 4:1-7). He, too, is growing in knowledge and understanding of his lady.

Tell Her She Is Beautiful (Song 6:4)

Solomon begins by saying to Shulammite, "You are as beautiful as Tirzah, my darling [ESV, "my love"], lovely as Jerusalem, awe-inspiring as an army of banners." These were two great and beautiful cities in that day. Lamentations 2:15 calls Jerusalem "the perfection of beauty, the joy of the whole earth." This woman's beauty was so captivating and power-ful to her husband that it was like he was looking at an awesome army with its banners in full display. Longman puts it well: "The beauty of the woman is so overpowering that it arouses fear as well as joy" (*Song*, 180). He sees beauty and strength in this woman.

Tell Her She Is Irresistible (Song 6:5-7)

Solomon is captivated by his wife's beauty. Bewitched! Under a spell! Her eyes are hypnotic, so he pleads with her, "Turn your eyes away from me." He then draws on prior descriptions of her, praising her hair (6:5), her teeth (6:6), and the beauty of her brow or cheeks, perhaps her temples (6:7). George Schwab says, "She singularly overwhelms the boy" ("Song," 414).

When I began dating Charlotte, some of my friends said I had been "caught in Charlotte's web!" They were right. Like Solomon, I was captivated, overwhelmed by her beauty. And I still am! Her eyes, her mouth, her face, and yes the rest of her, ensnared me and I have never been able to escape. The fact is, I have not wanted to. Why? Because I am hers and she is mine.

Tell Her She Is Special (Song 6:8-9)

This man wants this lady to know she is one of a kind. Special. Unique. As a lady, a woman of God, she transcends all others in his eyes. She is his standard of beauty. There is no lady like his lady.

In 6:8-9 he says there may be "60 queens and 80 concubines, and young women without number." None compare to her. She is his dove (1:15; 4:2; 5:2), his virtuous one (ESV, "perfect one"), she is unique (ESV, "the only one"). This favorable opinion is also shared by her mother and other women as well. Indeed they all "sing her praises" (6:9c).

Solomon is masterfully cultivating an environment of romance for his wife. No one compares to her. She is literally unique. All who know her bless her and praise her. Those who know her best love and admire her most, beginning with her husband. Tom Gledhill well says, "Happy is the girl who receives so much extravagant praise" (*Message*, 194). No doubt she is a happy girl. Her husband has seen to it.

Tell Her She Is Awesome (Song 6:10)

We are not certain of the speaker in verse 10. It could be Solomon, but most Old Testament scholars think it is the woman. There is no problem as to the meaning. All who know her see her in this light, her husband and everyone else. As a person and in appearance, four things are said about her: (1) she "shines like the dawn," (2) she is "as beautiful as the moon," (3) she is "bright as the sun," and (4) she is "awe-inspiring as an army with banners" (also 6:4). We might say she is celestial in her beauty and powerful in her presence. I love Duane Garrett's take on this verse, "In a Cinderella motif, the woman who was very ordinary is now extraordinary in her beauty and breathtaking to behold" (*Proverbs*, 418). Douglas O'Donnell simply adds, "She is out of this world" (*Song*, 102).

Practical Applications from Song of Songs 5:9–6:10

Marriage is hard work. It is also worthwhile work. One of the ways we work through difficult times is by seeking to bless our mates. This is a wonderful path to reconciliation, and it gives evidence of our Lord's redeeming work in our lives. As we have seen in our study, a woman has her part and a man has his part. What follows are some specific ways we can bless our spouses. Make sure to pay attention to your own responsibilities—let the Lord Jesus work on your mate!

Five Ways to Bless Your Husband

A wife can be a blessing to her husband by honoring him as the church honors Christ and giving him specific gifts of love:

1. Give him admiration and respect. As his wife, work to understand and appreciate his value and achievements. Remind him of his capabilities and gifts. Help him maintain his walk with God and also his self-confidence. Be proud of your husband, not out of duty, but as an expression of sincere admiration for the man you love and with whom you have chosen to share your life (Eph 5:22-23,33).

2. Provide sexual fulfillment. Become an excellent sexual partner to him. Study your own response to recognize and understand what brings out the best in you; then communicate this information to your husband, and together learn to have a sexual relationship that you both find repeatedly satisfying and enjoyable (Prov 5:15-19; Song 4:9–5:1; 1 Cor 7:1-5; Heb 13:4).

3. Cultivate home support. Create a home that offers him an atmosphere of peace and quiet and refuge. Manage the home and the care of the children. The home should be a place of rest and rejuvenation. Remember, the wife/mother is the emotional hub of the family (Prov 9:13; 19:13; 21:9,19; 25:24).

4. Strive to be an attractive wife. Pursue inner and outer beauty in that order. Cultivate a Christlike spirit in your inner self. Keep yourself physically fit with diet and exercise, wear your hair, makeup, and clothes in a way that your husband finds attractive and tasteful. Let your husband be pleased and proud of you in public, but also in private (Song 1:8-10; 2:2; 6:13–7:9; 1 Pet 3:1-5)!

5. Become his best friend. Develop mutual interests with your husband. Discover those activities your husband enjoys the most and seek to become proficient in them. If you learn to enjoy them, join him in them. If you do not enjoy them, encourage him to consider others that you can enjoy together. Become your husband's best friend so that he repeatedly associates you with the activities he enjoys most (Song 8:1-2,6).

Seven Ways to Bless Your Wife

A husband can be a blessing to his wife by loving her as Christ loved the church and giving her specific gifts of love:

1. Be a spiritual leader. Be a man of courage, conviction, commitment, compassion, and character. Take the initiative in cultivating a spiritual environment for the family. Become a capable and competent student of God's Word and live out before all a life founded on the Word of God. Lead your wife in becoming a woman of God, and take the lead in training the children in the things of the Lord (Ps 1; Eph 5:23-27).

2. Give her personal affirmation and appreciation. Praise her for personal attributes and qualities. Praise her virtues as a wife, mother, and homemaker. Openly commend her, in the presence of others, as a marvelous mate, friend, and companion. Help her feel that, to you, no one is more important in this world (Prov 31:28-29; Song 4:1-7; 6:4-9; 7:1-9).

3. Show personal affection (romance). Shower her with timely and generous displays of affection. Tell her how much you care for her with a steady flow of words, cards, flowers, gifts, and common courtesies. Remember, affection is the environment in which sexual union is enjoyed more fully and a wonderful marriage is developed (Song 6:10,13; Eph 5:28-29,33).

4. Initiate intimate conversation. Talk with her at the feeling level (heart to heart). Listen to her thoughts (i.e., her heart) about the events of her day with sensitivity, interest, and concern. Conversations with her convey a desire to understand her not to change her (Song 2:8-14; 8:13-14; 1 Pet 3:7).

5. Always be honest and open. Look into her eyes and, in love, always tell the truth (Eph 4:15). Explain your plans and actions clearly and completely because you are responsible for her. Lead her to trust you and feel secure (Prov 15:22-23).

6. *Provide home support and stability.* Take hold of the responsibility to house, feed, and clothe the family. Provide and protect, and do not feel sorry for yourself when things get tough. Look for concrete ways to improve home life. Raise the marriage and family to a safer and more fulfilling level. Remember, the husband/father is the security hub of the family (1 Tim 5:8).

7. *Demonstrate family commitment.* After the Lord Jesus, put your wife and family first. Commit time and energy to the spiritual, moral, and intellectual development of the children. For example, pray with them (especially at night by the bedside), read to them, engage in sports with them, and take them on other outings. Do not play the fool's game of working long hours, trying to get ahead, while your children and spouse languish in neglect (Eph 6:4; Col 3:19-20).

How Does This Text Exalt Christ?

There Is No King Like My King: How the King Loves His Bride!

The vision our bride has of her husband (5:10-16) is almost apocalyptic. It draws us to consider another vision in the last book of the Bible, the Revelation. There in 1:13-16 we see a vision of "One like the Son of Man," our great Shepherd-King, the Lord Jesus. Schwab notes we have here in our Song "an almost theophonic picture similar to Revelation 1:13-16. The young man is larger than life" ("Song," 410). I think he is exactly right. The young man is larger than life because he points us to Christ! Comparing Song of Songs 5:10-16 to Revelation 1:13-16, we see a magnificent description of Christ's head and hair, His eyes, His face, and His mouth. He is majestic and awesome, much like our bridegroom in the Song of Songs, but so much more. Interestingly, one can count ten features of the one being described both in Song of Songs 5:10-16 and in Revelation 1:13-16. There is no king like this King. He is larger than life and other-worldly. Again, Israel must have wondered, "I know the song is poetry, but will there ever be such a man, such a king, on this earth?" The good news of the gospel is yes! His name is Jesus!

And what about the bride? Oh how this king loves his bride! She is unique, his special possession. His praise for her is unparalleled. Why? Because he sees her as he has made her. He has imparted his life to her. He has given his heart to her and received hers in return. She is "my perfect one, the only one" (ESV, 6:9). He has sacrificed for her and sanctified her. He has been sensitive to her and he is satisfying to her. This is the love that this man has for his wife. This is the love that Christ has for His bride. Ephesians 5:25-33 runs through this Song, but it is especially evident here.

In our Song, the garden of Eden has been regained, but it anticipates even more. We wait for a king like no other. We long to be a bride loved like no other. For those who know Christ, what we long for has already arrived (Rom 5:10-11).

Reflect and Discuss

1. In what ways has God made provision for the troubles that we will encounter in any relationship?
2. How does this passage show the hard work it takes to have a healthy, biblical marriage? How do you need to work at your marriage to accurately display the gospel?
3. Why is it important for a husband and wife to cultivate a friendship? How can they do this?
4. Explain why sex is important to a healthy and vibrant marriage. Discuss 1 Corinthians 7:5 and the role sex plays in resisting temptation.
5. Why is it so important for a man to voice his love and affection for his wife? How does Solomon show his affection to Shulammite in 6:4-10?
6. What are some practical ways you and your spouse can "do your part" in reconciliation? How can you keep repentance and reconciliation as ongoing realities in your marriage?
7. Wives, which of the "Five Ways to Bless Your Husband" is something you could intentionally practice this week?
8. Husbands, which of the "Seven Ways to Bless Your Wife" is something you could intentionally practice this week?
9. Review the parallels between Song of Songs 5:10-16 and Revelation 1:13-16. What do these teach us about the risen Christ?
10. What does the love Solomon has for his Shulammite show us about Christ's affection for the church? How does he communicate his love to her?

The Kind of Man Every Woman Wants

SONG OF SONGS 6:11–7:10

Main Idea: A man in a gospel-saturated marriage will know his wife well so he can serve her well, continually pursuing intimacy "till death do us part."

I.   **Be Sensitive to Her Longings for Love (6:11-13).**
  A.   Watch how she acts (6:11).
  B.   Sense how she feels (6:12-13).
II. **Grow in the Knowledge of Your Mate (7:1-6).**
  A.   Grow in your knowledge of her physically (7:1-5).
  B.   Grow in your knowledge of her particularly (7:6).
III. **Remain Passionate in the Pursuit of Your Mate (7:7-10).**
  A.   Keep on expressing your desires for her (7:7-9).
  B.   Keep on receiving her affection for you (7:9-10).

A number of years ago I was scheduled to do an out-of-state Family Life conference. A week or so before I was to go, I received an anonymous card in the mail from a woman with a broken heart. Here is what she wrote:

> Dear Dr. Akin, I hope you receive my card before the marriage conference. . . . I recently married a member of our church. He will be attending your seminar. This past Valentine's Day he did not acknowledge the romantic holiday, and I was very hurt. I watched as my coworkers received flowers. To make things worse, he joked about it in front of one of my friends. My mom told me I should have known what to expect since he never gave me flowers while we were dating. This may sound selfish and petty on my part. I am just so discouraged! After I come home from my job, I do all the housework and cooking and shopping. I wouldn't mind so much if he would just occasionally show his appreciation. The only time he has ever given me a gift is on my birthday and Christmas. It would mean so much to me if just once he would give me something

151

just because he loves me. I exercise and try to look nice. I iron all his clothes and cook his favorite meals. He has thousands of dollars to invest in the stock market, but he has never spent one dollar on a romantic gift for me. I know flowers will eventually wilt, but they are so beautiful. I'm afraid my love will eventually wilt. Will you pray for me?

Every time I read that card my heart breaks for this wife. Her great pain is a daily reality. She has a husband who takes her for granted, and he probably doesn't even know how his wife feels. Whoever he is, he is failing miserably at obeying 1 Peter 3:7, where the Bible says to a Christ-following husband,

> *Live with your wives with an understanding of their weaker nature yet showing them honor.* (HCSB)

> *Live with your wives in an understanding way, showing honor to the woman as the weaker vessel.* (ESV)

> *Dwell with them according to knowledge, giving honour to the wife, as unto the weaker vessel.* (KJV)

In our Song we see a husband who knows his wife, understands his wife, and honors his wife. Here is a man who loves his wife as Christ loves His Church (Eph 5:25). Here is the kind of man every woman wants.

Be Sensitive to Her Longings for Love
SONG OF SONGS 6:11-13

Men are sexual creatures, but so are women. God made us this way by divine design. When there is friction in our relationship, things can get out of whack. Often, it is our intimate life that suffers. Solomon and Shulammite have been in the process of patching things up, of reconciling.

Now, in verses 11-13, we see the story of their reconciliation from the wife's perspective (Deere, "Song," 1022). She knew he was in the garden (6:2, a reference to a literal garden but also to her body), and so she joins him there. Solomon would be a wise man to watch how she acts and sense what she feels. Body language, tone of voice—these are female signals to which a man must be sensitive.

Watch How She Acts (Song 6:11)

Shulammite says, "I came down to the walnut grove . . . to see if the vines were budding and the pomegranates blooming." Again, a double entendre is probably at work here. She is looking for new and fresh evidences of their love in the grove. She knows he loves her. After all, look at what he said in 6:4-9. Still, she wants to be certain the offense of 5:2-8 has been forgiven. She wants to see for herself. So she, who is a garden, goes to the garden. Has Eden been restored?

Richard Hess believes her actions are clearly erotic and sensual: "The stroll around the garden is a stroll around the body of the lover [a reversal of the garden referent?]. It is a description of the beauty of the lover's body as well as suggesting the pleasures of love that await the speaker" (Hess, *Song*, 207). The wise husband would watch her actions carefully. Here, they are speaking loud and clear.

Sense How She Feels (Song 6:12-13)

All the commentators agree that verse 12 is the most difficult verse in the Song.[12] I like how Deere states the verse when he writes, "I became enraptured, for you placed me on the chariots of the people of the prince" ("Song," 1022; see also Gledhill, *Message*, 199). The HCSB rendering is not far from this: "Before I knew it, my desire put me among the chariots of my noble people." The idea is, I was overwhelmed, beside myself, with all that has happened (Garrett, *Proverbs*, 419). I feel like I have been swept off my feet by my king.

Verse 13 informs us that others are privy to this scene. They too are caught up in the moment and plead with her four times to "come back." She, however, is gone. The name "Shulammite," the feminine form of Solomon, appears only here in the Song. Literally it is "Solomoness," and it can mean "perfect one" (Garrett, *Proverbs*, 419).

They want her for a public viewing, but her husband wants her for a private viewing. He asks them, almost as a taunt, "Why are you looking at the Shulammite, as you look at the dance of the two camps," the dance of the Mahanaim? The exact meaning of this phrase is unclear, but her actions are not. They have praised her beauty, and she is appreciative.

---

[12] See Deere, 1022; Gledhill, 199.

But there is another whose praise means even more. That person is her husband. His praise has freed her to express herself with unhindered abandonment. She will now dance, and dance nakedly and seductively. However, this dance is not for many, but only for one. It will be a private performance reserved only for her husband. He has brought her to the bedroom because he sensed he could. He was right, and he will not be disappointed with what happens.

Grow in the Knowledge of Your Mate
SONG OF SONGS 7:1-6

For the third time in our Song the husband describes his wife. He did so previously in 4:1-7 and 6:4-10. Here, however, we have the most personal and detailed description of all. His words are more intimate and sensual. He will draw from his previous praises, but he will also advance into new territory. This would bless her heart. It would delight her soul.

There are a couple of valuable lessons here we must not miss. First, we cannot praise our mate too much or too often. This is especially true when it comes to a husband's need to praise his wife. It feeds and nourishes her (Eph 5:29). Second, we cannot know too much about our mate. In fact, a lack of knowledge and understanding of how she thinks and feels about certain things can be dangerous. It may approach the deadly! I learned this the hard way in our first year of marriage. It was a painful but memorable experience! We sat down one Saturday to eat sandwiches. As my wife Charlotte placed a wonderful sandwich on the table, she also put beside it a Tupperware container that had inside it, if you used your imagination and a magnifying glass, something that remotely resembled potato chips. Once these crumbs were placed in your mouth, you could easily have assumed it was a new variety of chewing gum. They were awful.

I turned to Charlotte and said, "Honey, I don't like these. They're too small and stale. I want some new fresh, crispy, potato chips." She responded, "Sweetheart, when all of these are gone, we can get some more."

That was not the answer I was looking for! I quickly responded, "But darling, I saw in the pantry on the way in here a brand new bag of fresh, crispy potato chips that has never been opened. I want those!"

Quick as a flash she shot back, "Well, sugar dumpling, when this container is empty, we can get those."

I then did something that a man would only do in his first year of marriage. I stood up, took her Tupperware, and dumped the chips on the floor! I then said, "This one is empty now. You can go and get the others."

It probably won't surprise anyone that she did not go get the other chips. It was rather chilly at our house (and in our bed) for several days, and I learned the danger of assuming I knew my wife and that she would appreciate my creative object lesson.

Just as I had much to learn about Charlotte, so we all must grow in our knowledge of our mate, and Solomon highlights two specific areas.

Grow in Your Knowledge of Her Physically (Song 7:1-5)[13]

Starting with her dancing feet and moving to a woman's glory, her hair (cf. 1 Cor 11:5), Solomon draws attention to and describes characteristics and features of his wife that he found attractive and beautiful. It is clear that she has removed her outer garment, and that she dances either in the light clothing of a shepherdess or fully naked. What follows favors the latter.

Solomon focuses on ten aspects of his wife's beauty. Though attention is on the physical, certain features also highlight the attractiveness of her personality and character.

She dances before him, and so he mentions first her feet. Her "sandals" (gentlemen, he noticed her shoes!) would have left the top of her feet nearly bare. This would have been alluring and particularly attractive (Snaith, *Song*, 100). His reference to her as a "princess" or "daughter of a nobleman" is a symbolic way of praising her noble character and testifies to how her husband viewed her and treated her. He honors her as God commands (again, see 1 Pet 3:7). There are no demeaning glances, no rude snapping of the fingers, no harsh words of contempt or criticism. She is a princess, a queenly maiden.

Her "thighs" are shapely ("curves") and priceless ("like jewelry"), the work of a skilled craftsman, "the handiwork of a master." The word refers to the upper part of the thigh where the legs begin to come together (Carr, *Song*, 156). Like priceless jewels they are attractive to see and precious to hold.

Verse 2 is badly translated in my judgment in virtually every English version. The problem is with the word translated "navel." It simply does not fit the upward progression or the description. The Hebrew word

---

[13] This section draws heavily from Akin, *God on Sex*, 213–15.

is rare, occurring only three times in the Old Testament (cf. Prov 3:8; Ezek 16:4). Here the word almost certainly is a reference to the inner-most sexual part of a woman, her vagina (vulva) (see Carr, *Song*, 157; Snaith, *Song*, 101). Solomon's description makes no sense of a navel, but it beautifully expresses the sexual pleasures he continually receives from his wife. Like "a rounded bowl; it never lacks mixed wine"—she never runs dry. She is a constant source of intoxicating pleasure and sweetness. The idea of blended or "mixed" could refer to the mingling of male and female fluids in the appropriate place of a woman's body (Snaith, *Song*, 103). Shulammite was an exotic garden (4:12,16) and an intoxicating drink (7:2) in her lovemaking. Seldom, if ever, was her husband disap-pointed. She was his dream lover, and amazingly, he wasn't dreaming! The more he learned about her the more he loved and enjoyed her.

In verse 3 he compares her waist to "a mound of wheat surrounded by lilies." This could refer to her gentle curved figure and also to the fact she was like food to him. She is wheat and wine, food and drink. She nourishes and satisfies him as he has sought to nourish and satisfy her.

He again describes her breasts "like two fawns" (cf. 4:5). They are soft and attractive, enticing him to pet them. Her neck (7:4) is an ivory tower (cf. 4:4). She is majestic, stately, a confident and dignified lady. Her eyes are beautiful, pure and refreshing (cf. 1:15; 4:1), like the Moabite city of Heshbon (cf. Num 21:25), a city known for its reser-voirs. The location of Bath-rabbim is unknown, though it is possible that the gate in Heshbon led to the pools. Her nose is "like the tower of Lebanon looking toward Damascus." She is strong in character and there is a genuine sense in which he draws strength and security from her. He may also be saying "her nose complements and sets off her facial beauty" (Garrett, *Proverbs*, 422).

Her "head crowns [her] like Mount Carmel" (v. 5). The Carmel range was considered one of the most beautiful in all of Palestine. She is beautiful and remarkable, majestic and awesome (cf. Isa 35:2; Jer 46:18). Her hair is "like purple [or deep red] cloth," and her husband is "held captive" by its beauty. He has been ensnared by her. A king has been captured. The more he knows her, the greater is her hold on him.

Grow in Your Knowledge of Her Particularly (Song 7:6)

Solomon summarizes his detailed description of Shulammite by again telling her how beautiful she is (cf. 7:1). This forms something of an inclusio to his song of praise in this section. It adds weight and emphasis to his declaration of her beauty. He then tells her "how pleasant" she is, "my love, with such delights!"

This wife is beautiful in his eyes and she pleases him. Her delights—note the plural—are many, some of which he just listed. Garrett points out this verse is best read as "daughter of delights" (i.e., "delightful woman") (*Proverbs*, 422). Everything about her, every detail, every particular of her person, is a delight, a joy, a blessing to his soul. The more he knows her the more he loves her.

Noting that it is the king who is speaking and in view here, George Schwab says, "Before the charms of the formidable lady, the otherwise sovereign ruler is held fast and helpless. . . . It is because she is so delightful that she captivates the king" ("Song," 419). This is a remarkable lady indeed. She is not the same shy and insecure girl we first met in 1:5-7. The love of her king has transformed her!

Remain Passionate in the Pursuit of Your Mate
SONG OF SONGS 7:7-10

In recent years research on marriage and family has revealed some interesting facts. To a secular-minded culture the conclusions proved surprising. To those of us committed to a biblical worldview, what was discovered was not surprising at all. It was found that "the most emotionally and physically satisfying sex was between committed partners." Furthermore, "emotional and physical satisfaction from sex increases with sexual exclusivity, with emotional investment in the relationship, and a longtime horizon for the relationship" (Greeley, "Privileging").

The husband and wife in the Song of Songs would say to us, "We already knew this! We learned this in the real life laboratory of marriage, and what a joy it is to share what we learned." A persistent passion for your mate is a healthy tonic for a happy, growing relationship. So as you move forward growing old together, keep a couple of things in mind.

Keep On Expressing Your Desires for Her (Song 7:7-9)

Solomon compares his wife to a stately, swaying palm tree (v. 7). It would seem she has continued her seductive dance and he is mesmerized. He also tells her that "her breasts are clusters of fruit." They are an attractive, sweet, and tasty fruit that he finds irresistible. In verses 8-9 he quickly and passionately expresses his desires for her: "I said, 'I will climb the palm tree and take hold of its fruits.'" He then adds, "May your breasts be like clusters of grapes, and the fragrance of your breath like apricots [or "apples"]. Your mouth is like fine wine." Everything about her entices him. Their love has not grown stale.

It is time for the dance to end and lovemaking to begin (again). Solomon has watched his wife dance naked before him as long as he can. His passion for her is at a fever pitch and he tells her so. He is picturesque in his description of her, but he is also direct in his desire for her. Her body, her breasts, her breath, and her mouth are all objects of his desire and passion.[14] That he describes her mouth like "fine wine" recalls the fact that Shulammite said the same about his mouth in 1:2. He is glad to return the compliment as they enter into intimacy. Theirs is a sweet and intoxicating love.

In our day we too speak of beautiful, graceful palm trees. This is what this husband sees in his wife, and he must have her. Schwab says with frankness, "After mounting the palm tree, he will vigorously denude its fruit. . . . The girl delights in his designs and expresses her desire to see that his foretastes are not disappointed" ("Song," 420). This leads us to our final observation.

Keep On Receiving Her Affection for You (Song 7:9-10)

John Gries says, "Jesus intended marriage to be happy for you. God expects regular sex in marriage, and sex is a learning process" (Lackey, "Counselor Offers Help"). Gries is right, and we have seen this truth lived out in our Song. This couple has grown in their knowledge of each other. They have learned both how to give and how to receive.

Shulammite gladly gives herself to Solomon in response to his request, and he, no doubt, is happy to receive her gift of lovemaking. Picking up on the imagery of wine, Shulammite expresses her desire to satisfy and bring pleasure to her husband. The wine flows "smoothly for my love," she says, "gliding past my lips and teeth!" The NKJV says, "The wine goes down smoothly for my beloved, moving gently the lips of sleepers" (i.e. the lovers). They are making love to one another and it is delightful—like sweet, intoxicating wine. They exchange kisses and intimate expressions of love that each finds satisfying, and then they restfully fall to sleep in a warm embrace. His goal is to satisfy and please

---

[14] Carr (*Song*, 162–63) notes that breath could be a reference in the Hebrew language to the nipples of her breasts. Garrett (*Proverbs*, 422) concurs.

her, which he does. Her goal is to satisfy and please him, which she does. When there is mutual giving with the goal of pleasing our mate, the marvelous result is that both spouses experience the joy and pleasure God intended (cf. 1 Cor 7:3-4; Phil 2:3-5).

Practical Applications from Song of Songs 6:11–7:10

PROVERBS 32: THE HUSBAND OF NOBLE CHARACTER

A husband of noble character: who can find one? He is worth more than winning the Publisher's Clearinghouse Sweepstakes or the lottery.

His wife has full confidence in him and she lacks nothing of importance.

He brings her good, not harm, all the days of her life.

He works hard to provide for his family. Getting up early he helps get the children ready for school, then dashes off to work.

With his shoulder to the grindstone he works with energy and vigor, as one who is working for the Lord (Col 3:23). And while busy, he always finds time to call his wife during the day just to say, "I love you."

He promptly comes home from work and immediately pitches in with the chores, helping the children with their homework, or with making dinner if he can cook! While hot dogs and baked beans are his specialty, he doesn't fear the microwave, remembering nothing metal should be in there. He does this with such ease that all are amazed and in awe.

When his wife prepares a meal he always eats with gusto, and when finished, he never forgets to smile and tell her how great the meal was. Of course, he is always the first to volunteer to do the dishes or at least to volunteer the children to complete the task!

All in all, he is a joy to have in the kitchen.

As a father, there is no equal on the face of the earth. No matter how exhausted from work or chores, he always takes time for his children.

Whether it's making funny faces at the baby, tickling the small child, wrestling with the kids, watching football with his sons, or making pained and disbelieving expressions at his teenagers, he is always there for them.

He is a whiz at math, science, spelling, geography, Spanish, and any other subject his children are studying at school.

And if he should be totally ignorant of the subject at hand, he skillfully hides his ignorance by sending the child to their mother.

He can fix any problem, from a scraped knee to loose bicycle chains, from interpreting rules for a kickball game to refereeing sparring matches between his kids.

More importantly, he is also the spiritual leader in the family. He loves Jesus, and he always takes the family to church. He shows his children, by his example, what it means to be a man of God.

He teaches his children how to pray and the importance of knowing and loving the Lord Jesus. He often rises early to pray for his wife and children, and he reads from his Bible at night before sleeping.

He disciplines his children with loving firmness, never by yelling or with humiliating words. He is always more interested in teaching a lesson than in simply punishing.

During the day he meditates on God's Word and on how to live it. He shows Christ in all his dealing with others and is considered a valuable employee by his bosses. His co-workers respect his hard work, his integrity, and his kindness.

He always shows his wife the utmost respect, even opening the door for her. He is always quick with a word of encouragement, and is constantly telling her how beautiful she is, even when she isn't wearing any make-up.

A day seldom passes that he doesn't tell her of his love for her. Praise for her is always on his lips.

Anniversaries and birthdays are never forgotten and gifts and flowers are often given, "just because."

He even makes superhuman efforts to be nice when her family is visiting.

He is full of compassion for the pain of others and willingly helps those in need. Whether it's changing a stranger's flat tire, helping with a friend's home improvement project, or feeding the poor at the local soup kitchen, he is the first to volunteer.

He is not afraid to shed a tear with a friend in pain or to be rowdy in laughter at another's joke.

He loves life and lives it with passion.

His children, while not always calling him "blessed," have no doubts about his great love for them. His wife also calls him many things, among them, "the best man there is," and she thanks God for him.

Many men do great things but he surpasses them all. There is no man better than this man, except Jesus.

Flattery is deceptive and good looks, like hair, is fleeting, but a man who fears the Lord is to be praised. Give him the reward he has earned, and let his deeds bring him praise. His Lord is pleased, his wife loves him, and his children are proud of him. He is a blessed man indeed.[15]

How Does This Text Exalt Christ?

How the King Sees His Bride

The king (7:5) in our text sees his bride as beautiful (7:1,6). She belongs to him, and his desire is for her (7:10). He sees her as virtually flawless, with no imperfection (4:7). Of course she is not literally flawless and perfect. There has never lived on this earth such a bride. I guess a good question to ask is, will there ever be such a bride?

Well, the good news, gospel answer, is "yes!" There will indeed be such a bride that will not only appear perfect, she will be perfect. This will not be an earthly bride, but a heavenly one, one made perfect by the Bridegroom who has cleansed her by His blood and made her pure and spotless from head to toe. Once more our Song prepares us for the awesome and glorious truth of Ephesians 5:25-27: "Christ loved the church and gave Himself for her to make her holy, cleansing her with the washing of water by the word. He did this to present the church to Himself in splendor, without spot or wrinkle or anything like that, but holy and blameless."

This is what this bride is destined to be, and the good news of the gospel is, you can be a part of this bride. Repent of sin and look in faith

---

[15] Adapted and revised version of a poem by Michael M. Jones, a former student at Southern Seminary in Louisville, Kentucky, 1996.

to the Bridegroom, King Jesus, who loved you and gave Himself for you. His love for you is great. His cleansing power cannot fail. He longs to make you beautiful. He longs for you to be His.

> Come, ye sinners, poor and needy,
> Weak and wounded, sick and sore;
> Jesus ready stands to save you,
> Full of pity, love, and pow'r.

> I will arise and go to Jesus,
> He will embrace me in His arms;
> In the arms of my dear Savior,
> Oh, there are ten thousand charms.
> 　　　(Hart, "Come, Ye Sinners")

Reflect and Discuss

1. What are some things men allow to distract them from honoring their wives? Wives, discuss how this failure makes you feel.
2. Shulammite wants to confirm that Solomon still loves her deeply. What can husbands do to communicate this clearly?
3. Why is it so important to praise your mate? What are the dangers of failing to do so?
4. What value is there in knowing your mate physically?
5. Do you find yourself shocked at the explicitness of 7:1-6? Discuss how this passage fits into the purpose of the whole Bible.
6. Why do you think pleasure and satisfaction in marriage increase with time and commitment? How does this go against the grain of popular culture?
7. How can husband and wife approach sexual intimacy with the goal of pleasing the other person? Why does this lead to more satisfaction for both?
8. Consider the poem on the Proverbs 32 husband. Husbands, what are some points of application for your life?
9. Wives, which of these qualities in a husband are most desirable to you? Why?
10. The perfection of this woman prefigures the perfected church in the resurrection. What are some of the characteristics of this perfected church, and how can the church today seek to display those characteristics?

The Kind of Woman Every Man Wants

SONG OF SONGS 7:10–8:4

Main Idea: Wives in a gospel-saturated marriage will play their part in initiating, cultivating, and sustaining intimacy in a way that reflects the church's devotion to her King, the Lord Jesus.

I. **Be Aggressive When It Comes to Intimacy (7:10-13).**
   A. You tell him you are his (7:10).
   B. You make the arrangements (7:11-13).
   C. You be creative (7:13).
   D. Twelve Ways to Keep Passion Alive in Your Marriage
II. **Be His Friend as Well as His Lover (8:1-2).**
   A. Public displays of love will bless him (8:1).
   B. Private displays of love will delight him (8:2).
III. **Be Faithful in Your Devotion to Him (8:3-4).**
   A. Receive his advances and embrace (8:3).
   B. Declare your convictions and commitment (8:4).

Biblical marriage is under attack—severe attack—in our day. As a result, many of our children run the risk of growing up confused and even wrongheaded when it comes to rightly understanding this God-ordained institution. In an article titled "5 Truths Children Won't Know about Marriage Unless We Teach Them," author Linda Kardamis says,

> Marriage is under attack in our culture. From the sexual revolution to the rise of divorce to the fight over same-sex marriage, this precious institution is being bombarded from all sides.
>
> And our children are right in the middle of it.
>
> Hollywood, the media, our school systems, and sometimes even fellow Christians are constantly portraying an untrue version of marriage to today's children and teens. And it's taking its toll.
>
> Most girls spend lots of time imagining their fairy tale wedding yet know very little about how to actually build a happily-ever-after. . . .

We are failing to give the next generation a proper perspective on marriage. A perspective they desperately need. But we can change that. We can start talking to our kids, grandkids, Sunday school class, and youth group about this important institution. They need to grow up with a firm foundation in this area. It's not something they can just start working on *after* they say "I Do." (Kardamis, "5 Truths")

Kardamis then highlights five specific truths that must be taught and must be passed on to the next generation.

5 Truths We Must Teach Children about Marriage

1. God designed marriage to be between a man and a woman. We cannot be intimidated in this fight for God's design for marriage. God's Word is clear that marriage is for one man and one woman. He loves all people despite their sin, and we should do the same. But that doesn't mean we must accept all forms of ungodly behavior. Our children are being taught by the world that homosexuality is just as valid as traditional marriage. We need to teach them that it's not. God's way is always best.

2. Marriage is a life-long commitment. When we promise "for better or worse" we give our solemn vow. It's not "for better or for worse unless things get really bad" or "to love and to cherish unless I stop loving them" or even "till death do us part unless they cheat on me." Marriage is a covenant relationship that is meant to last a lifetime. Often we as Christians are scared to openly discuss this because we don't want to offend those who have been hurt by divorce. But those who have gone through a divorce would likely be the first to tell you what heartache and pain it causes. And those whose spouse walked out on them certainly wish their spouse's parents had instilled in them that divorce should not be an option.

3. Marriage is worth waiting for. Contrary to every other voice in our culture, God's Word still teaches that sex is a gift to be enjoyed exclusively within the bonds of marriage. If we aren't actively teaching this to our teens, they will quickly be persuaded otherwise. But the physical relationship isn't the only area where waiting is important. They must also be patient in waiting for the right person. . . .

4. Marriage is not about being compatible. Much of the focus on relationships in our society is about being compatible, but the truth is that no two people are compatible 100% of the time. . . . Marriage, while incredible, takes a lot of work, sacrifice, and adjustment. I think lots of marriages break up because no one is teaching young people this concept. So they expect that everything will be wonderful, and at the first sign of trouble they assume they married the wrong person and decide they want out.

5. Marriage is about giving, not receiving. Marriage is not about what our spouse does for us. It's about what we can do for them. It's not about feeling loved or appreciated. It's about making someone else feel loved and appreciated. The next generation needs to step into marriage ready to give, regardless of whether or not they receive. But this truth, I'm afraid, only means so much when we talk about it. This one, I fear, has to be taught by example. (Kardamis, "5 Truths")

There is real wisdom here, especially when it comes to her last statement about being "taught by example." In Song of Songs 7:10–8:4 we are blessed with an awesome example of what it means to be a godly woman and a wonderful wife. Here we see a lady who is the kind of woman every smart man wants, the kind of woman Jesus Christ redeemed and that He is sanctifying His spiritual daughters to be. The portrait that follows is quite a lady! Any man would be a lucky man to call her his wife.

Be Aggressive When It Comes to Intimacy
SONG OF SONGS 7:10-13

An available and aggressive wife, when it comes to intimacy, is a blessing and delight to her husband. Most men would agree with Matt Sess who said concerning his wife, "When she initiates sex, it's definitely a turn on. . . . It doesn't happen a lot, but when it does, it's a pleasant surprise" (Walsh, "Who's Lighting the Fire?").

Thankfully more and more women, especially Christian women, are feeling free to be the aggressor when it comes to lovemaking. There is nothing wrong about this and everything right about it. The fact is, it has biblical warrant! Watch and observe our beautiful lady Shulammite in these verses.

You Tell Him You Are His (Song 7:10)

Shulammite beautifully declares concerning her relationship to her husband, "I belong to my love, and his desire is for me." The word translated "desire" is an important one. It is found elsewhere only in Genesis 3:16, where it speaks of a wife's desire for her husband, and in Genesis 4:7, where it speaks of sin's desire to control Cain. In both contexts "desire" appears to be viewed negatively. Here in our Song, the idea of desire is clearly positive. The curse is reversed and we once more find ourselves in Eden.

It is also interesting to see how Shulammite changed what she said from two previous statements in our Song. Note the comparison:

My love is mine and I am his. (2:16)

I am my love's and my love is mine. (6:3)

I belong to my love, and his desire is for me. (7:10)

Jack Deere sums up the progression so well:

[His] desire is for me. This is a more emphatic way of stating possession. How much more could a husband belong to his wife than for him to desire only her? She had so grown in the security of his love that she could now say that his only desire was for her. She had been so taken by his love for her, that she did not even mention her possession of him. (Deere, "Song," 1023)

Shulammite's complete and total focus is on her king. For her, it is more than enough to be his and the person he desires. "I belong to you and I know you want me." This prepares us for the next step.

You Make the Arrangements (Song 7:11-13)

Shulammite now takes the initiative for lovemaking and invites her husband for a weekend getaway to the country. She is spontaneous and she is enticing. She knows sex that takes place only at home in the familiar can run the risk of becoming just a routine. Vacations, weekend getaways, and "one nighters" can often enhance and even rekindle the passions in marriage. She invites her man to leave the city and go with her. And she repeats the invitation!

> *Let's go to the field; let's spend the night. . . . Let's go early to the vineyards; let's see if the vine has budded.*

Again using the imagery of springtime, our lady invites her husband for some personal time away and alone where she promises, "There I will give you my love" (7:12). Budding vines, blossoms opening, pomegranates in bloom, and "mandrakes" (7:13) were all considered aphrodisiacs in that day. Lloyd Carr tells us that mandrakes were referred to by some as the "love apple" (*Song*, 165).

In the countryside, out of doors, under the stars and moon, amid sweet, sensual smells, Shulammite promises a night of romantic lovemaking. She will take care of everything. All he has to do is show up!

Charlotte and I have a dear friend named Barbara O'Chester. She has spoken to thousands of women about marriage, sex, and romance. She points out that sometimes women struggle in the area of romance and sexual pleasure and she notes at least ten possible and common reasons:

1. Ignorance
2. Resentment
3. Guilt
4. Physical Problems (illnesses)
5. Fear
6. Passivity
7. Hormones
8. Weight Problems
9. Fatigue
10. Lack of Time

Song of Songs provides some real assistance in overcoming a number of these. Are you fatigued? Take a vacation. Do you lack time? Get away. Do as verse 13 directs: at the door of your mate, find "every delicacy." Lay your inhibitions aside and let your imagination run wild.

You Be Creative (Song 7:13)

Because of the way God has wired both a man and a woman, "At our door *is* every delicacy" (emphasis mine). In other words our God has given us everything we need physically, mentally, and emotionally to share a lifetime of intimacy that never grows old or stale. One key to this ongoing romance is found in the last phrase of verse 13: "new as well as old." Indeed Shulammite tells her husband, "I have treasured them up for you, my love."

As we spend years together in marriage, God's plan is that things mature and grow sweeter. As we learn how to love our mate well, we will discover some pleasures and joys that never grow old. They are so good we just keep on repeating them. And as we move forward in life together, we will discover new pleasures and joys as well. Now discovering new pleasures and joys does not usually happen by accident. We have to be intentional. We have to work at it. So here are some ideas to consider along these lines.

Twelve Ways to Keep Passion Alive in Your Marriage

1. Work at it. A lifetime of love and romance takes effort. Few things in life are as complicated as building and maintaining an intimate, passionate relationship. You need to work on it constantly to get through those trying periods that require extra work.

2. Think team. When making important decisions, such as whether to work overtime or accept a transfer or promotion, ask yourself this question: What will the choice I am making do to the people I love? Talk with your mate and family. Make "we" decisions that will have the most positive impact on your marriage and your family.

3. Be protective. Guard and separate your marriage and your family from the rest of the world. This might mean refusing to work on certain days or nights. You might turn down relatives and friends who want more of you than you have the time, energy, or wisdom to give. You might even have to say no to your children to protect time with your spouse. The kids won't suffer if this is done occasionally and not constantly. It will actually be beneficial for everyone!

4. Accept that good and not perfect is okay when it comes to your mate. No one is perfect other than Jesus! You married a real person who will make real mistakes. However, never be content with bad. Always aim for great, but settle for good!

5. Share your thoughts and feelings. We have seen this one over and over. Unless you consistently communicate, signaling to your spouse where you are and getting a recognizable message in return, you will lose each other along the way. Create or protect communication-generating rituals. No matter how busy you may be, make time for each other. For example, take a night off each week, go for a walk together on a regular basis, go out to breakfast if you can't have dinner alone, or just sit together for 30 minutes each evening simply talking, without any other distractions.

6. Manage anger and especially contempt better. Try to break the cycle in which hostile, cynical, contemptuous attitudes fuel unpleasant emotions, leading to negative behaviors that stress each other out and create more tension. Recognize that anger signals frustration of some underlying issue. Avoid igniting feelings of anger with the judgment that you are being mistreated. Watch your non-verbal signals, such as your tone of voice, hand and arm gestures, facial expressions, and body movements. Remain seated, don't stand or march around the room. Deal with one issue at a time. Don't let your anger about one thing lead you into showering the other with a cascade of issues. If different topics surface during your conflict, note them to address later. Try to notice subtle signs that anger or irritation is building. If you are harboring these feelings, express them before they build too much and lead to an angry outburst. Keep focused on the problem, not persons. Don't turn a fairly manageable problem into a catastrophe. Emphasize where you agree.

7. Declare your devotion to each other again and again. True long-range intimacy requires repeated affirmations of commitment to your spouse. Remember: love is in both what you say and in how you act. Buy flowers. Do the dishes and take out the trash without being asked. Give an unsolicited back or foot rub. Committed couples protect the boundaries around their relationship. Share secrets with each other more than with any circle of friends and relatives.

8. Give each other permission to change. Pay attention. If you aren't learning something new about each other every week or two, you simply aren't observing closely enough. You are focusing on other things more than one another. Bored couples fail to update how they view each other. They act as though the roles they assigned and assumed early in the relationship will remain forever comfortable. Remain constantly abreast of each other's dreams, fears, goals, disappointments, hopes, regrets, wishes, and fantasies. People continue to trust those people who know them best and who love and accept them.

9. Have fun together. Human beings usually fall in love with the ones who make them laugh, who make them feel good on the inside. They stay in love with those who make them feel safe enough to come out to play. Keep delight a priority. Put your creative energy into making yourselves joyful and producing a relationship that regularly feels like recess.

10. Make yourself trustworthy. People come to trust the ones who affirm them. They learn to distrust those who act as if a relationship were a continual competition over who is right and who gets their way. Always act as if each of you has thoughts, impressions, and preferences that make sense, even if your opinions or needs differ. Realize your spouse's perceptions will always contain at least some truth, maybe more than yours, and validate those truths before adding your perspective to the discussion.

11. Forgive and forget. Don't be too hard on each other. If your passion and love are to survive, you must learn how to forgive. Ephesians 4:32 must always be front and center. You and your spouse regularly need to wipe the slate clean so that anger doesn't build and resentment fester. Holding on to hurts and hostility will block real intimacy. It will only assure that no matter how hard you otherwise work at it, your relationship will not grow. Do what you can to heal the wounds in a relationship, even if you did not cause them. Be compassionate about the fact that neither of you intended to hurt the other as you set out on this journey.

12. Cherish and applaud. One of the most fundamental ingredients in the intimacy formula is cherishing each other. You need to celebrate each other's presence. If you don't give your spouse admiration, applause, appreciation, acknowledgement, the benefit of the doubt, encouragement, and the message that you are happy to be there with them now, where will they receive those gifts? Be generous. Be gracious. One of the most painful mistakes a couple can make is the failure to notice their own mate's heroics. These small acts of unselfishness include taking out the trash, doing the laundry, mowing the lawn, driving the carpool, preparing the taxes, keeping track of birthdays, calling the repairman, and cleaning the bathroom, as well as hundreds of other routine labors. People are amazingly resilient if they know that they are appreciated. Work hard at noticing and celebrating daily acts of heroism by your mate (source unknown; see Akin, *God on Sex*, 222–26).

Be His Friend as Well as His Lover
SONG OF SONGS 8:1-2

These two verses can sound rather strange to modern, Western ears, but they would have been sweet music to Solomon's. They would have let him know that the love that his wife had for him was multifaceted and multidimensional. Their relationship is more than romantic lovemaking, though it was not less than this. Theirs is a covenantal relationship that involves loyalty, sacrifice, and most importantly, friendship. A man needs a best friend and he needs that best friend to be his wife. Shulammite evidently understood this, and so she takes the necessary steps to make it happen.

Public Displays of Love Will Bless Him (Song 8:1)

Shulammite wishes that she could treat Solomon like a blood relative, like a brother, "like one who nursed [just like she did] at my mother's breasts." If that were the case, "I would find you in public [not just in private] and kiss you, and no one would scorn [ESV, "despise"] me."

Jack Deere again helps us unravel what we read here when he says, "In the ancient Near East public displays of affection were frowned on except in the case of certain family members" ("Song," 1023). I would point out that is still true in many places. A brother would be an acceptable candidate for public affection, even kissing, and Shulammite wishes she had the freedom anyplace and anytime to show the world her love and affection for her man. She will not reject or cast aside accepted social behavior and expectations, but she sure would like to! No, she will not subject herself or her husband to public scorn, ridicule, or contempt. She will restrain her actions, but her intention is loud and clear: Yes, you are my lover, but you are also like my brother, like my friend. Wonderfully in Christ, a husband and a wife truly are brother and sister! Such is the power and goodness of the gospel!

Private Displays of Love Will Delight Him (Song 8:2)

It seems that Shulammite begins to be playful with her husband in this verse (Deere, "Song," 1023). Assuming the role of an older sister, she tells him, "I would lead you, I would take you to the house of my mother who taught me." And once she got him there what would she do? "I would give you spiced wine to drink from my pomegranate juice." The word for "lead" in Hebrew refers to "a superior leading an inferior: a general, his army; a king, his captain; a shepherd, his sheep. . . . She would lead her younger brother to their common home" (Glickman, *Song*, 90).

Shulammite notes it was at home that she was taught and received instruction from her mother. In the context, she must mean instruction about matters of sexual intimacy and love. This is a valuable lesson, especially for those of us who are parents. "The art of preparing for love is best learned at home" (Carr, *Song*, 167). Dads and moms must take charge at appropriate times and in appropriate ways in teaching their children about the birds and the bees. They cannot leave this vital task in the hands of others. They dare not entrust it to a locker room and girlfriend talk. Dads must instruct their sons and mothers must guide their daughters. This does not mean dads have no part in training their daughters or moms in assisting their sons, but gender often will play a role in who takes the lead with whom.

Shulammite informs Solomon of some things she learned from her mother. "Spiced wine," special wine, would be on their lover's menu as well as the juice of her pomegranate. "An ancient Egyptian love poem identifies a wife's breasts with the fruit of the pomegranate" (Carr, *Song*, 157). Duane Garrett points out that the reference to her "mother's house" could easily be a euphemism for the intimate sexual parts of the woman (*Proverbs*, 425). That the overtones of her words are sensual and erotic is undeniable. The joy of lovemaking that they share does not wane. It grows more intensive and creative as their marriage progresses. And much of the credit lies at the feet of Shulammite.

Be Faithful in Your Devotion to Him
SONG OF SONGS 8:3-4

In an article entitled "Nourishing Your Love," Marie Pierson advises women on how to touch a man's heart. Her six suggestions:

1. **Show him admiration and appreciation.** Let him know he is your hero and champion.
2. **Nurture his friendship.** Work to become his best friend. He truly wants that. In fact, he needs it.
3. **Lower your expectations.** You married a real person! He is a sinner just like you.
4. **Watch your priorities.** Is he number one after Jesus?!
5. **Enhance your love life.** Continue to grow as a creative, passionate, and sensual lover.
6. **Be forgiving** . . . even as God in Christ has forgiven you (Eph 4:32). (Adapted from Pierson, "Nourishing.")

It appears Shulammite understands these suggestions quite well. She knows how to love her man in ways he will understand and appreciate. Two things, in particular, stand out in these final verses of our study.

Receive His Advance and Embrace (Song 8:3)

"His left hand is under my head, and his right hand embraces me."
Solomon gently and tenderly is holding and caressing his wife. Perhaps
they have just finished making love and they rest in each other's arms
in the afterglow of the moment. He does not leap out of bed and run
downstairs for a snack. She doesn't slip out of bed to make a quick
phone call, nor does she rush out of the room to attend to unfinished
chores. They simply lie there loving each other and holding each other.
They are tender in their affections. We have been here before (cf. 2:6).
By God's goodness and grace they will return here again and again and
again. He longed to hold and caress her. She was delighted and happy
to receive those caresses.

Declare Your Convictions and Commitment (Song 8:4)

For the third and final time (cf. 2:7; 3:5) the importance of the proper
time and the proper person for lovemaking is addressed. Obviously God
believes timing is important. First, the right time for lovemaking is only
in marriage between a man and a woman. Second, within marriage,
timing and sensitivity to the needs and feelings of our mate is crucial
as we build and nurture affection and romance. Shulammite declares
both her convictions concerning this issue and her commitment. Song
of Songs 8:10-12 will bear eloquent witness that she indeed lived out
what she believed. She blessed her husband on their wedding night with
a chaste and pure bride who would give herself to her husband passionately until separated by death.

Some popular pundits say that modern Christian advice concerning
sex dates back to 1973 and a book by Marabel Morgan entitled *The Total
Woman.* Actually, advice for Christians concerning sex goes all the way
back to the book of Genesis when, prior to the fall, Adam and Eve "were
naked, yet felt no shame" (Gen 2:25). We find the climax of God's counsel in the Song of Songs. Here we discover that our God says sex and
romance are good *in marriage.* Indeed they are essential. It is encouraging to see that more and more Christians "see sex more as a gift to be
enjoyed within marriage than as an evil to be endured or avoided," and
that "an orthodox view of romance, courtship, and sexuality" may be
the best road to sexual satisfaction (Michael, Gagnon, Laumann, and
Kolata, *Sex in America,* 113). Solomon worked at doing his part. In these
verses we have seen Shulammite doing her part. My only regret to this
discovery is this: Why hasn't it always been this way? After all, God's plan

for the Christian bedroom has never changed. It is a good thing. It is a great thing. Yes, it is a God thing.

Practical Applications from Song of Songs 7:10–8:4

The love shared by our couple in this Song is a wonderful thing to behold. It truly is "new as well as old" (7:13). Below are some biblical principles to help our love never to grow stale, always to be fresh. There is some very good discussion material here.

Yardsticks for Love
(OR, HOW TO MEASURE LOVE)

1. Love responds to the total person, not just to the physical. (Gen 2:22-24; Prov 31:10-31)
2. Love respects and holds in high esteem the one loved. (Eph 5:28-29)
3. Love gives of itself to enrich and benefit the other person. (Eph 4:15-16; 5:25-27)
4. Love is willing to assume responsibility. (John 10:11; Heb 12:2)
5. Love rejoices in being together and suffers pain in separation.
6. Love can bear separation(s). (1 Cor 13:4-5)
7. Love can forgive and forget the other person's mistakes. (1 Cor 13:5,7; Eph 4:32)
8. Love patently aids the other in correcting his or her faults. (Eph 4:2,29)
9. There is in love the mutual enjoyment of each other without physical expression.
10. Love has a protective attitude. (John 10:11-13)
11. Love has a sense of belonging to the other person. (Gen 2:23-24)
12. Love grows and matures. (Eph 4:15-16)
13. Love is gentle and kind; it always behaves. (1 Cor 13:4-6)
14. Love feels undeserving of the other person.
15. Love waits for the proper time for physical expression and for marriage. (Heb 13:4)
16. Love guards the other person's moral purity. (1 Cor 13:6; Eph 5:25-27; Heb 10:24)
17. Love bears the wounds and pains inflicted by the other person. (1 Cor 13:5,7; Eph 4:32)

18. Love seeks to assist the other person in becoming even more special. (all of the above) (Sauer, *Romance* packet)

How Does This Text Exalt Christ?

I Want to Go Home with My King!

There are two ideas in this passage that naturally lead us to meditate on what we have in Messiah Jesus. One we see directly and the other by contrast.

First, Shulammite says she wishes she could treat her shepherd-king like her brother, like a very close intimate friend. Well, the good news of the gospel is that not only can our Shepherd-King Jesus be treated like a brother, He *is* our brother! In Hebrews 2:11 we are told that those who have been saved and call God their Father have a Savior who also, "is not ashamed to call them brothers" (also Heb 2:12,17). What a wonderful truth! The One who is my Savior, Lord, Master, and King is also my brother. I have a brother who is a King! He is my King. What Shulammite wishes for in Solomon we have in Jesus.

Second, Shulammite informs Solomon she would be delighted if she could take him home "to the house of my mother" (8:2). Here is a bride taking the bridegroom to her home. Well, for those who are in Christ, just the opposite will someday take place. The Bridegroom will take His bride to His home, to an eternal home He has prepared just for her. In John 14:1-3 the Lord Jesus said to His disciples, "Your heart must not be troubled. Believe in God; believe also in Me. In My Father's house are many dwelling places; if not, I would have told you. I am going away to prepare a place for you. If I go away and prepare a place for you, I will come back and receive you to Myself, so that where I am you may be also." What amazing grace! I truly do "belong to my love, and his desire is for me" (Song 7:10). He has redeemed me and some day He will take me to His house—"His Father's house"—where we will live together forever and ever. With His left hand under my head and His right arm embracing me (8:3), I am safe and secure. He will never let me go. This is our brother. This is our lover. This is the great Shepherd-King who has a love for us that "mighty waters cannot extinguish" (8:7). This bride in our text is remarkable indeed. She is what she is because her king loves her the way that he does. One question remains: Do you want to go home and live forever with King Jesus? He is preparing a home for all who do, and someday He will take us there.

Reflect and Discuss

1. Give some examples of where you have seen the attack on biblical marriages in our culture.

2. Consider the "5 Truths" to teach children about marriage. Discuss why these are so important and the consequences of failing to communicate them.

3. Wives, what are some barriers that prevent you from initiating intimacy? What are some practical ways you can take initiative with your husband?

4. Why must we work to keep passion alive in marriage? Why doesn't it just happen naturally?

5. Discuss how forgiveness relates to maintaining passion and intimacy. What passages of Scripture might speak to the need for forgiveness in our relationships?

6. How can couples work at being friends as well as lovers? Talk with your spouse about how public and private displays of affection can communicate friendship and love.

7. Why do you think the proper time and person for sexual intimacy is brought up again and again in the Song?

8. Why do you think some people have a hard time seeing sex within the bounds of marriage as a good gift from God?

9. Which of the "Yardsticks for Love" are revealing to you? What do they say about your marriage?

10. What does it mean that "what Shulammite wishes for in Solomon we have in Jesus"? What does it *not* mean?

A Love That Lasts Forever

SONG OF SONGS 8:5-14

Main Idea: The gospel shapes marriage in such a way that the love shared by husband and wife extends grace to both and reflects the love between Christ and His bride, the church.

I.   Cultivate a Love That Is Public (8:5).
II.   Cultivate a Love That Is Private (8:5).
III.   Cultivate a Love That Is Personal (8:6).
IV.   Cultivate a Love That Is Protective (8:6).
V.   Cultivate a Love That Is Possessive (8:6).
VI.   Cultivate a Love That Is Passionate (8:6).
VII.   Cultivate a Love That Is Persevering (8:7).
VIII. Cultivate a Love That Is Priceless (8:7).
IX.   Cultivate a Love That Is Pure (8:8-9).
X.   Cultivate a Love That Is Peaceable (8:10).
XI.   Cultivate a Love That Is Privileged (8:11-12).
XII.   Cultivate a Love That Is Permanent (8:13-14).

Love is a wonderful thing. It is a very important thing. This is certainly the perspective of our God who directly addresses the subject several times in Scripture. We can immediately think of Matthew 22:34-40, where Jesus says the two great commandments are to love God and love your neighbor as yourself. We can immediately think of John 13:35, where Jesus says, "By this all people will know that you are My disciples, if you have love for one another." We can immediately think of the beautiful "love chapter" of 1 Corinthians 13, where we learn that God's kind of love "never ends" (v. 8). And we can immediately think of 1 John 4, where we are reminded that "God is love" (vv. 8,16).

Yes, love is a wonderful and important thing, but it can also be a confusing and misunderstood thing, especially in the context of romance. Too often people think they are in love when actually they are only infatuated with another person. Making this mistake can be disastrous. How, then, can we tell the difference between the two? I came across a short comparison some years ago that contrasts the two. It really helps bring clarity to the issue.

"Love or Infatuation"

Infatuation leaps into bloom. Love usually takes root and grows one day at a time.

Infatuation is accompanied by a sense of uncertainty. You are stimulated and thrilled but not really happy. You are miserable when he is absent. You can't wait until you see her again. Love begins with a feeling of security. You are warm with a sense of his nearness, even when he is away. Miles do not separate you. You want her near. But near or far, you know she is yours and you can wait.

Infatuation says, "We must get married right away. I can't risk losing him." Love says, "Don't rush into anything. You are sure of one another. You can plan your future with confidence."

Infatuation has an element of sexual excitement. If you are honest, you will discover it is difficult to enjoy one another unless you know it will end in intimacy. Love is the maturating of a friendship. You must be friends before you truly can be lovers.

Infatuation lacks confidence. When he's away, you wonder if he's with another girl. When she is away, you wonder if she is with another guy. Sometimes you even check. Love means trust. You may fall into infatuation, but you never fall in love.

Infatuation might lead you to do things for which you might be sorry, but love never will. Love lifts you up. It makes you look up. It makes you think up. It makes you a better person than you were before. (Adapted from Landers, "Infatuation or Love?")

There can be no doubt that the Song of Songs also thinks love is important. The theme runs throughout its eight chapters and 117 verses, but it reaches a climax in the final chapter. Twelve different characteristics of the love God cultivates between a man and a woman in covenant marriage are addressed in 8:5-14. Here we will see that love truly is "a many splendored thing." Here we will discover "a love that lasts forever!"

Cultivate a Love That Is Public
SONG OF SONGS 8:5

For the second time in our song we read the phrase, "Who is this coming up from the wilderness" (cf. 3:6). Schwab says, "The wedding of the great king is reenacted in the [public] passion of the twosome; the kingly celebration serves as an example for all lovemaking" ("Song of Songs," 425). Here are Solomon and Shulammite riding again in the royal chariot in full public display. She reclines, relaxed and secure, "leaning on the one she loves." "Coming up from the wilderness" recalls the time of Israel's 40 years of wandering before entering the promised land. This couple has passed through those "wilderness periods" in their marriage and safely arrived on the other side. The wilderness also conveys the idea of the fall and its curse (see Gen 3; see also Jer 22:6; Joel 2:3). Their love relationship is a redeemed relationship through God's grace. The effects of the fall and the Genesis curse (Gen 3:16-19) have been reversed and the disharmony that sin brings into a relationship has been overcome. This is what Jesus Christ can do when He is Lord of our marriage. Frederica Matthews-Green says, "Women need men to call us up toward the highest moral principles; [men] need [women] to call them down to the warmth of human love and respect for gentler sensibilities. . . . It's clear that we need each other. You would almost think someone planned it that way" ("Matters of Opinion"). The love that this king and his bride enjoy is something all the world should see and learn from.

Cultivate a Love That Is Private
SONG OF SONGS 8:5

Our scene suddenly shifts from the chariot to the "apricot" (or apple) tree, from the public to the private. Once more the wife has initiated lovemaking. Under the tree of romance and sexual intimacy, "the sweetheart tree of the ancient world" (Glickman, *Song*, 96) Shulammite awakens her lover, saying that it is "there your mother conceived you; there she conceived and gave you birth." This is a beautiful example of Hebrew parallelism.

Duane Garrett points out that the bride-to-be "calls her beloved an apple [or apricot] tree in 2:3 and thus the figure of his mother being 'under the apple tree' means that his mother was with his father.

Similarly, the place where his mother conceived and gave birth to him refers to the female parts. . . . The woman means she and he are now participating in the same act by which the man himself was given life" (Garrett, *Proverbs*, 426). It is important to see that the passion and desire for sexual intimacy is still aflame in their marriage. Their private time alone in the bedroom has not grown cold or stale. Again we see that what takes place outside the bedroom impacts what takes place inside the bedroom. In that private sanctuary, he initiates lovemaking and she initiates lovemaking. Clearly, the king continues to "take pleasure in the wife of [his] youth" (Prov 5:18) and Shulammite does the same with her husband. We should, by God's grace, grow old together, but our love should never grow old.

Cultivate a Love That Is Personal
SONG OF SONGS 8:6

The wife asked her husband to "set me as a seal on your heart." A person's seal, here the seal of the king, was extremely important and personal. Jack Deere notes, "In Old Testament times a seal was used to indicate ownership of a person's valued possessions. So the beloved asked to be the lover's most valued possession" ("Song," 1024).

She wants to be a seal, but one placed in a very particular and personal location: "on your heart." In the ancient world it was often the custom to wear a signet ring or cylinder on a cord or necklace around the neck and near the heart. Schwab notes, "To be imprinted as a seal on another is to be inseparable from that person. She wishes his life to be hers" ("Song," 426). For the king to love his lady in such a way that she felt near and dear to his heart would speak personally of his undying devotion and lasting love. As long as his heart beats, she wants to know and feel his love.

Believers in Jesus have a King who has set His seal on us, emblazoning it on our foreheads (cf. Rev 9:4) as a personal pledge of possession and protection. And we did not even have to ask. Indeed, through salvation provided for us in Christ, our God has "sealed us and given us the Spirit as a down payment in our hearts" (2 Cor 1:22). We have His seal on our foreheads and His seal in our hearts. We are "double-sealed" by our great Shepherd-King. The personal and intimate love He has for those who belong to Him is a pledge and promise we should never doubt.

Cultivate a Love That Is Protective
SONG OF SONGS 8:6

This wife also wants to be set as a seal on her husband's arm. The idea is one of safety, security, and strength. If the seal on the heart spoke of that which is deep and inward, the seal on the arm spoke of that which is public and external. It would be analogous to our wedding rings today (O'Donnell, *Song*, 117).

True love will always have a protective attitude and disposition toward one's mate. You will want them to feel safe and secure in the strength of your love. You will work mightily to guard them, protect them, shield them from anyone or anything that could damage, harm, or injure them. You will be their defender to whom they can always run for rest and refuge.

Now let me make a specific application at this point. It is very important. One of the most lethal weapons in a relationship is the little chipping at one another with hurtful and sarcastic barbs. This is deadly when done in front of others. You develop and encourage a person by magnifying their strengths, not their weaknesses. Take pride in your mate. Praise your mate. Learn to protect your mate, especially with your words.

Cultivate a Love That Is Possessive
SONG OF SONGS 8:6

The word *for* tells us that the rationale for the previous statements in verse 6 is about to be given. Why does Shulammite want Solomon to set her as a seal on his heart and on his arm? "For love is as strong as death; ardent love is as unrelenting as Sheol [or, the grave]." The phrase "ardent love" is translated "jealousy" in a number of translations. What is Solomon saying here?

"Love is as strong as death" means it is universal and irresistible. It is going to get you! Indeed, ardent, intense, zealous, jealous love swallows down men and women once it has laid hold of them just as personally and possessively as does Sheol, death, and the grave. Paige Patterson says, "In godly love a righteous jealousy is as hard or inevitable as the grave" (*Song*, 117). It will not let go. There is a permanent possessiveness to the kind of love God gives to the godly man and woman in marriage. "Lovers are defenseless when in its grasp" (Schwab, "Song," 426).

There is a popular saying in the world of athletics that says, "When the going gets tough, the tough get going." That statement may be true. However, of one thing I am certain because the Bible says so: "When the going gets tough, love keeps going." It refuses to quit, drop out of the race, throw in the towel, or let go of its lover. It is strong and unrelenting. As Paul says in 1 Corinthians 13:7-8, "It bears all things, believes all things, hopes all things, endures all things. Love never ends."

Cultivate a Love That Is Passionate
SONG OF SONGS 8:6

This is a fascinating and much debated phrase. The variations in its translation bear this out:

> *Love's flames are fiery flames—fiercest of all.* (HCSB)

> *Its flashes are flashes of fire, the very flame of the LORD.* (ESV, NASB)

> *It burns like blazing fire, like a mighty flame.* (NIV 1984)

> *Its darts are darts of fire—divine flame.* (CEV)

> *Love flashes like fire, the brightest kind of flame.* (NLT)

> *Its flashes are flashes of fire, a most vehement flame [the very flame of the Lord]!* (AMP)

Now why do some translations have the words *Lord* or *divine* in them and some do not? It is because in the Hebrew Bible on the word translated "flame" there is a suffix *-yah*, which could possibly be a shortened form of the divine name *Yahweh*. If this is correct, and I am inclined to think that it is, then the Lord God Himself, *Yahweh*, is the source of this mighty, fierce, blazing, passionate love (see also the HCSB marginal reading). The kind of love ignited and fueled by the Lord is a fervent flame, a blazing fire. As we will see in verse 7, nothing can extinguish this love. Like a raging forest fire, it burns with such intensity that no one can control it. It is a passionate, God-given, red-hot flame that will endure any and all efforts to put it out.

Such a passionate love is the kind of love our Shepherd-King, our divine Bridegroom, has for us. His is a "great love that He had for us" (Eph 2:4). Indeed, He "loved me and gave Himself for me" (Gal 2:20). His is truly a passionate love "that surpasses knowledge" (Eph 3:19). As the recipients of such a fervent, passionate love, let us, in passionate loving response, "be imitators of God. . . . And walk in love, as the Messiah also loved us and gave Himself for us" (Eph 5:1-2).

Cultivate a Love That Is Persevering
SONG OF SONGS 8:7

And You Wonder Why It Didn't Last

She married him because he was such a "strong man."
She divorced him because he was such a "dominating male."

He married her because she was so "fragile and petite."
He divorced her because she was so "weak and helpless."

She married him because "he knows how to provide a good
     living."
She divorced him because "all he thinks about is business."

He married her because "she reminds me of my mother."
He divorced her because "she's getting more like her mother
     every day."

She married him because he was "happy and romantic."
She divorced him because he was "shiftless and fun-loving."

He married her because she was "steady and sensible."
He divorced her because she was "boring and dull."

She married him because he was "the life of the party."
She divorced him because "he never wants to come home
     from the party." (Van Buren, "And You Wonder")

God designed marriage to last. Jesus said, "Therefore, what God has joined together, man must not separate" (Matt 19:6). Marriage is not for a season. It is not like leasing a car. It is meant for a lifetime. Solomon says the love that God gives is so passionate and powerful, "Mighty waters cannot extinguish it; rivers cannot sweep it away." Tom Gledhill puts it so well as he describes what he calls "the indestructibility of love":

For though water can quench any flame, there are no hostile
forces which can quench the flame of love. It is inevitable
that love will always be tested and tried, will always encounter
forces that threaten to undermine and destroy it. These may

be the outward circumstances that may erode love's power: the pain of separation, the uncertainty of the present or future, the loss of health or means of livelihood. But the love which is fuelled by the energy of God will triumph and overcome all these adversities and will emerge purer and stronger and more precious through the testing. (Gledhill, *Message*, 234)

In Isaiah 43:1-2 the words that our Lord speaks to His people remarkably parallel these words in our Song. It again reminds us that the love we've seen on display between this man and woman mirrors and points to a greater love, the love our redeemer God has for a people He has chosen for Himself. What did our Lord say through His prophet?

> *Now this is what the LORD says—the One who created you, Jacob, and the One who formed you, Israel—"Do not fear, for I have redeemed you; I have called you by your name; you are Mine. I will be with you when you pass through the waters, and when you pass through the rivers, they will not overwhelm you. You will not be scorched when you walk through the fire, and the flame will not burn you."*

Cultivate a Love That Is Priceless
SONG OF SONGS 8:7

Real love, true love, cannot be bought. It has no price tag. It is not for sale. Craig Glickman is right: "By its very nature love must be given. Sex can be bought, love must be given" (*Song*, 101). Solomon tells us, "If a man were to give all his wealth for love, it would be utterly scorned." The ESV says, "He would be utterly despised." Try to buy love, he says, and prepare to be publically ridiculed and mocked. Prepare to become a laughingstock.

What are some clear and practical steps we can take to maintain and nurture this divine treasure deposited in our marital bank account by our lavishly generous heavenly Father? I appreciate the suggestions of a lady named Joanna Weaver. Some of these are a real challenge. All are worth considering.

25 Ways to Love Your Lover

1. List the top 10 reasons I'm the most fortunate husband or wife in the world. Read them aloud to your spouse.

2. Surprise your mate by doing one of his or her chores. When asked why, give a smooch and say, "because you are worth it."
3. Don't just show—tell! Say, "I love you."
4. Communicate your plans to each other. On Sunday night, go over your schedules for the coming week.
5. Use the T.H.I.N.K. method to determine whether an issue needs to be brought up. Is it true? Helpful? Important? Necessary? Kind?
6. Plan an appreciation celebration for your mate, complete with his or her favorite meal.
7. Look at your schedule. Make time with your spouse a weekly priority.
8. Bring back those dating days. After bringing the sitter, walk back outside and knock on the door with flowers in your hand.
9. Don't turn on the TV until after dinnertime, if at all. Wait for a conversation to break out.
10. Pray together. Thank God for your mate, then pray for his or her special needs.
11. On your spouse's birthday, send your in-laws a thank-you card.
12. Set boundaries in outside relationships. Don't let anyone take away too much of the time you spend with your spouse.
13. Are you seeing eye-to-eye? Experts have found that the deeper the love shared between spouses, the more frequent the eye contact.
14. Pull out old love letters, taking turns reading and reminiscing.
15. Take turns reading the Bible each night.
16. Stretch out birthdays with special activities, fun surprises, and a whole lot of hoopla.
17. Be a student of your spouse. Learn what he likes. Learn what she needs.
18. Treat your wife like a lady. Open doors and hold chairs.
19. Throw away fighting words like "You never . . ." and "You should . . ." Use healing words like "I'm sorry" and "You might be right."
20. Make church attendance a joyful priority.
21. Instead of making a joke at your spouse's expense, give a sincere compliment.
22. Create traditions as a couple by budgeting money for special times together.

23. Be affectionate. Back rubs and tender hand-holding communicate love.
24. Choose your battles carefully.
25. Be a person of integrity. Give your spouse no reason to doubt your word or question your commitment. (Weaver, "25 Ways")

Cultivate a Love That Is Pure
SONG OF SONGS 8:8-9

Verses 8-12 are not easy to interpret. Good, godly Bible scholars admit their difficulty and also draw different conclusions. This is what I think is going on.[16] Verses 8-12 probably should be understood as a flashback to Shulammite's youth and her initial meeting of Solomon. She grew up in a family where her brothers had been hard on her (1:6), but they were also protective. They watched over her and gave attention to her moral development and maturity. Even at a young age when she was "a little sister" (ESV) who had "no breasts" they kept an eye out for her as they considered the time when she would give herself to a man in marriage. "If she is a wall" speaks of moral purity and sexual unavailability. If she demonstrates such character they will honor her as a tower of silver, "a silver parapet." She would be given freedom and responsibility. On the other hand, "if she is a door," indicating moral and sexual vulnerability and weakness, they would enclose her and board her up in order to protect her. If she is irresponsible and reckless in her moral conduct and sexual behavior, they "will enclose [her] with cedar planks." They will wisely, and of necessity, restrict her freedom and opportunities for sexual foolishness and misbehavior.

Saving yourself sexually for marriage and giving yourself as a virgin to your mate may be out of style and old-fashioned in our sex-crazed culture, but it honors the Lord who redeemed you and it will bless the mate you wed. It will not be easy, but it is worth the commitment. How do you reach this lofty goal? A few ideas to consider:

1. Remember that your body is the temple of the Holy Spirit and that you have been bought at a price, the precious blood of Christ (1 Cor 6:19-20).

---

[16] See Deere, "Song," 1024–25. My views are very similar to his.

2. Remember that you are to glorify God in everything that you do (1 Cor 10:31).
3. Pursue holiness and purity (1 Pet 1:15-16).
4. Avoid the places of temptation and run from them (1 Cor 6:18).
5. Discipline your thought life by daily immersing yourself in God's Word, seeking to develop the mind of Christ (Prov 23:7; Rom 12:1-2; 1 Cor 2:16; Phil 2:5).

A final and important word on this point: it is never too late to pursue moral purity both *before* and *in* marriage. It is never too late to begin doing the right thing. In the gospel there is grace, forgiveness, and power. No sin, including sexual sin, is beyond the Savior's redeeming and healing love.

Cultivate a Love That Is Peaceable
SONG OF SONGS 8:10

Shulammite gives a personal testimony concerning her personal, moral purity and the blessing it was to her husband. She boldly declares, "I am a wall," meaning I was a virgin when we married. Now, as a vibrant, mature, and sensual woman ("my breasts are like towers"), "in his eyes I have become like one who finds peace." The word for "peace" is *shalom*, meaning completeness, well-being, wholeness. Purity equals peace in the marriage equation. Because of the faithful, pure, holy, and godly woman that she is, her man sees her as *shalom*, one who brings peace to their relationship. Mutual delight, joy, and well-being are the fruit of what was once a virgin garden, but now it is his garden to enjoy in peace (4:14–5:1).

This woman made this man complete, whole. She was that divinely sent companion, the helper who is his complement (Gen 2:18,20). In her presence he finds peace; he is set at ease. For him, the wall comes down and her towers fall into his hands. His banner over her is love (2:4), and her banner over him is peace (8:10). O'Donnell says it well: "His victory over her virginity (ironically) brings peace—to her, to him, to them, to everyone around them" (*Song*, 129). So we see in marriage holiness is a path to happiness. Purity is a path to peace, just another gift ultimately provided by the Prince of Peace, our Lord Jesus Christ (Isa 9:6-7).

Cultivate a Love That Is Privileged
SONG OF SONGS 8:11-12

As noted earlier, these are difficult verses to interpret. The precise meaning is vague, and Bible teachers are all over the place in how to understand the text. It seems to me that the main point is to show that Solomon, who was blessed with great wealth, had the right and privilege to administer his possessions in any way that he chose. Shulammite, though limited in her resources, had the same rights and privilege. This is especially true when it comes to giving her body ("my vineyard") to a man in marriage.

Solomon "owned a vineyard at Baal-hamon" (location unknown). The name could be translated "lord of abundance," which is an apt description of Solomon's great wealth. "He leased the vineyard to tenants," with the expectation of a 5-to-1 profit margin. For every 1,000 pieces of silver brought to Solomon, the tenants would receive 200.

Shulammite also had a vineyard: her body (cf. 1:6). She belongs to no one except the one to whom she chooses to give herself. Solomon may own thousands of possessions, but she is given as a gift. Again, we are reminded that love cannot be bought; it can only be given. It is a privilege, not an obligation, to give your body to another, to give yourself to another person. Never lose sight of the truth that you are blessed and privileged to receive the affection and love of your mate. You cannot earn it and you really do not deserve it.

Do you ever look at your mate and think, "God gave her to me?" "God finely crafted this man for me?" You should. True love always has the quality of a gift. After all, God loved the world by giving His only Son (John 3:16).

Cultivate a Love That Is Permanent
SONG OF SONGS 8:13-14

These two verses constitute a fitting conclusion to the Song of Songs. Appropriately, both the man and the woman speak, with the woman having the final word! These verses recall the days of spring. Shulammite is in the garden, she who is herself a garden (4:12). Friends or companions are listening for her voice. She is a popular and much loved lady. And yet she belongs to only one man, and he is the one who wants above all others to hear her voice. His words express both urgency and passion: "Let me hear you." This is an exclusive request. It is a specific request.

She responds with words we have heard before (cf. 2:8,17): "Make haste, my beloved, and be like a gazelle or young stag" in mating season. Hurry and enjoy "the mountains of spices," a reference no doubt to her breasts (2:17; 4:6). Only her lover is welcome there, and he is always welcomed there.

The mention of the garden again takes us back to Eden, to a time when the marital relationship had not been damaged or tarnished by the fall. Throughout our song Genesis 1–2 is in view, not Genesis 3 and all the heartache that followed the first couple's sin. Here at the end, the love this couple shares is still passionate. Indeed, by all indications, it is permanent. It will endure because it has its source in God (8:6). It will endure because it is focused on the other and not on one's self. She dwells in the garden. This is her home. This is where she lives. Her husband is called to join her there and to enjoy all the delights marriage offers. He will not look for female companionship anywhere else. Why would he? In his lovely lady he has found all that he could ever dream or hope for.

Practical Applications from Song of Songs 8:5-14

We began our study contrasting love and infatuation. Let's conclude in the same way. Below is a simple comparison provided by Josh McDowell. It is very applicable to teens and those who think they may have found their life partner, their "soul mate." Read and think through the list very carefully. Don't rush. Really contemplate what is here.

What's the Difference between Love and Infatuation?

Infatuation has been defined as "the emotional impulse of love, untested by time or circumstance." Since infatuation can lead to real love, sometimes it is difficult to see the difference. The characteristics in the chart below show the difference between infatuation and real love.

The Fairy Tale—Infatuation	The Real Thing—Love
• Fall into it suddenly	• Grows with time
• Deepens little with time	• Always deepening
• Wants sex now	• Willing to wait for sex
• Up and down emotionally	• Consistent
• In love with love	• In love with a person
• Fickle	• Faithful
• Can't eat or sleep	• Has proper perspective
• Hostile break-up at the slightest irritations	• Does not panic when problems arise
• Emphasizes beauty	• Emphasizes character
• Gets	• Gives
• Based on my feelings	• Based on other's needs
• Self-centered	• Self-controlled
• Shows emotion	• Shows devotion
• Physical	• Spiritual
• Expects to find happiness	• Expects to work at happiness
• Asks, "How am I doing?"	• Asks, "How are you doing?"
• Focuses on the performance of the other person	• Provides unconditional acceptance of the other person
• May feel this way toward more than one person	• Feels this way toward one person
• Possessive	• Allows the other person to relate to others
• May be based on few contacts (only person you've dated)	• Based on many contacts (dated many others)
• Has an idealized image of the other person	• Has a realistic view of the other person's strengths and weaknesses
• Avoids problems	• Works through problems (McDowell, "What's the Difference?")

How Does This Text Exalt Christ?

The Coming of the King!

Our song ends with the bride asking her shepherd-king to again come be with her (8:14). Interestingly, the Bible ends in exactly the same way. In Revelation 22 the bride twice asks for the Bridegroom to come to her and for her (22:17,20). Then and only then will God's great love song and story be complete. Only then will it reach its intended goal. The Song of Songs ends by pointing us to that great day and the climax of history.

I really cannot improve on the words of Douglas O'Donnell, as he describes so well what the end of our song should engender in our hearts:

> It is my contention and others' that this ending leaves us longing for more. In other words, the Song intentionally ends abruptly and inconclusively because the Song is not done. Love is not done. God is not done with his great love song and story. The Song of Songs ends with this eschatological angst. What's going to happen next? . . .
>
> In Revelation 22:20, this is how the book ends, how the Bible ends: in the last chapter and verse of our Bibles, our Lord Jesus/the Bridegroom says, "Surely I am coming soon," and the Church/the bride says, "Come" (v. 17), "Amen. Come, Lord Jesus!" (22:20). Make haste! That's how the Bible ends. That's how the Song ends.
>
> So *virginity* and *eschatology* is what we have here. And what do both topics have in common? Waiting. . . . Waiting for marriage; waiting for the marriage of the Lamb. Today we, as the Church, the bride of Christ, join the bride of the Song of Songs and her final plea. As we eagerly await the return of Christ (see Hebrews 9:28), "the descendant of David, the bright morning star" (Revelation 22:16), we hold our hands out with eschatological angst, knowing that only in the return and absolute reign of King Jesus can "the yearning for love [that] fills the cosmos" be met, consummated in and through and for the glory of Christ. The Apostle Paul puts it like this:
>
> "For the grace of God has appeared, bringing salvation for all people, training us to renounce ungodliness and worldly passions, and to live self-controlled, upright, and godly lives in the present age, *waiting* for our blessed hope, the appearing of the glory of our great God and Savior Jesus Christ" (Titus 2:11-13 ESV).
>
> And so we wait. (O'Donnell, *Song*, 132)[17]

---

[17] O'Donnell quotes John Updike, "Foreword," in *The Song of Solomon: Love Poetry of the Spirit*, ed. Lawrence Boadt (New York: St. Martin's, 1999), 9.

Reflect and Discuss

1. How would you explain the difference between love and infatuation? Why is it helpful to make this distinction?

2. What are the dangers of a love that is merely private? What are the dangers of a love that is merely public?

3. What will a healthy protection look like in marriage? What are some things you can do to protect your spouse and your marriage from harm?

4. Sometimes being "possessive" of another person is misunderstood and misused. What does being possessive in marriage *not* mean, and what does a healthy possessiveness look like?

5. How can couples persevere in love when the tough realities of marriage hit? What passages of Scripture support your ideas?

6. What is it about the nature of love that means it cannot be purchased? How does this relate to the gospel story?

7. True peace and *shalom* are powerful ideals for marriage in a fallen world. How can couples pursue and cultivate peace on a regular basis?

8. If receiving love is such a privilege, as 8:11-12 seems to suggest, why is it so easy for us to become complacent in marriage? How can you tell when love is being taken for granted in a marriage?

9. Why is marital love meant to be permanent? How does this conflict with our culture's views of marriage?

10. Discuss how the end of the Song parallels the end of Revelation and how this affects our interpretation of the Song.

WORKS CITED

Akin, Daniel. *God on Sex: The Creator's Ideas about Love, Intimacy, and Marriage* (Nashville: B&H, 2003).

Boice, James Montgomery. *Psalms: Volume 2 (42–106)*. Grand Rapids: Baker, 1994).

Bombeck, Erma. *Family—the Ties That Bind and Gag!* New York: Fawcett, 1988.

Bourke, Dale Hansen. "Motherhood—It Will Change Your Life." *Dale Hansen Bourke* (blog). Accessed March 14, 2014. http://www.dale hansonbourke.com/1/post/2013/05/it-will-change-your-life.html.

Carr, G. Lloyd. *The Song of Solomon*. Tyndale Old Testament Commentaries. Downers Grove: IVP, 1984).

Chapman, Gary. *Toward a Growing Marriage: Building the Love Relationship of Your Dreams*. Chicago: Moody, 1985.

Cicero, Marcus Tullius. "The Speech for Aulus Licinius Archias, the Poet." Translated by C. D. Yonge. Accessed December 17, 2013. http://www.forumromanum.org/literature/cicero/arche.html#26.

CNN. "Grisham ranks as top-selling author of decade." December 31, 1999. Accessed January 1, 2014. http://archives.cnn.com/1999/books /news/12/31/1990.sellers/index.html.

Constable, Thomas. "Notes on Song of Solomon, 2014 Edition." *Dr. Constable's Expository (Bible Study) Notes*. Accessed January 28, 2014. http://www.soniclight.com/constable/notes/pdf/song.pdf.

Crosby, Robert, and Pamela Crosby. *Now We're Talking: Questions to Build Intimacy with Your Spouse*. Colorado Springs: Focus on the Family, 1996.

Dalton, Patricia. "Daughters of the Revolution." *Washington Post*, May 21, 2000.

Danby, Herbert, trans. *The Mishnah: Translated from the Hebrew with Introduction and Brief Explanatory Notes*. 1933. Reprint, New York: Oxford University Press, 1967.

Deere, Jack S. "Song of Songs." In *The Bible Knowledge Commentary: An Exposition of the Scriptures by Dallas Seminary Faculty*, edited by John F. Walvoord and Roy B. Zuck, 1009–1025. Wheaton: Victor, 1985.

Dillow, Linda, and Lorraine Pintus. *Intimate Issues: Twenty-One Questions Christian Women Ask about Sex*. Colorado Springs: Waterbrook, 1999.

Driscoll, Mark. "His Garden." Sermon preached at Mars Hill Church, Seattle, October 2008. Accessed January 28, 2014. http://marshill.com/media/the-peasant-princess/his-garden.

Edwards, Jonathan. "The Church's Marriage to Her Sons, and to Her God." In *The Works of Jonathan Edwards*, 2:17–26. Reprint, Carlisle, PA: Banner of Truth, 1979.

Elias, Marilyn. "Marriage Makes for a Good State of Mind." *USA Today*, August 14, 2000.

Eller, T. Suzanne. "Berry Mauve or Muted Wine?" In *Chicken Soup for the Couple's Soul*, edited by Jack Canfield, et al. Deerfield Beach, FL: Health Communications, 1999. Used by permission of the author.

Elliot, Elisabeth. *Trusting God in a Twisted World, and Other Reflections on Asking God Why*. Grand Rapids: Revell, 1989.

Garrett, Duane. *Proverbs, Ecclesiastes, Song of Solomon*. NAC 14. Nashville: Broadman, 1993.

Gledhill, Tom. *The Message of the Song of Songs*. The Bible Speaks Today. Downers Grove: IVP, 1994.

Glickman, S. Craig. *A Song for Lovers: Including a New Paraphrase and a New Translation of the Song of Solomon*. Downers Grove: InterVarsity, 1976.

Goodnow, Cecilia. "Phil McGraw Draws Raves for 'No Bull' Approach to Rescuing Relationships." *Seattle Post-Intelligencer*, March 4, 2000: 195.

Greeley, Andrew. "'Privileging' Marriage." *Smart Marriages*. August 6, 2000.

Griffiths, Paul J. *Song of Songs*. Brazos Theological Commentary. Grand Rapids, MI: Brazos, 2011.

Hamilton, James M., Jr. "The Messianic Music of the Song of Songs: A Non-Allegorical Interpretation" *Westminster Theological Journal* 68 (2006): 331–45.

Harlow, John. "Brides Vow: I Do, until I Don't." *Free Republic Online*. August 5, 2005. Accessed January 29, 2014. http://www.freerepublic.com/focus/f-news/1457235/posts.

Hess, Richard S. *Song of Songs*. Baker Commentary on the Old Testament Wisdom and Psalms. Grand Rapids: Baker Academic, 2005.

Hubbard, David A. *Ecclesiastes, Song of Solomon*. Communicator's Commentary 15b. Dallas: Word, 1991.

Jay, Meg. "The Downside of Cohabitating Before Marriage." *New York Times*. April 14, 2012. www.nytimes.com/2012/04/15/opinion/sunday/the-downside-of-cohabiting-before-marriage.html?page wanted=all&_r=0.

Kardamis, Linda. "5 Truths Children Won't Know about Marriage Unless We Teach Them." *Patheos*. September 26, 2013. Accessed February 20, 2014. http://www.patheos.com/blogs/faithwalkers/2013/09/5-truths-children-wont-know-about-marriage-unless-we-teach-them.

Keel, Othmar. *The Song of Songs*. Continental Commentary. Minneapolis: Fortress, 1994.

Kinlaw, Dennis. "Song of Songs." In *Expositor's Bible Commentary*, edited by Frank E. Gaebelein, 5:1199–2244. Grand Rapids: Zondervan, 1991.

Lackey, Terri. "Counselor Offers Help to Couples for Reclaiming Marriage Intimacy." *Baptist Press*. November 1, 2000.

Landers, Ann. "Infatuation or Love? A World of Difference." *Chicago Tribune News*. April 18, 1998. Accessed February 26, 2014. http://articles.chicagotribune.com/1998-04-18/news/9804180019_1_dear-ann-landers-column-piano.

Longman, Tremper, III. *Song of Songs*. NICOT. Grand Rapids: Eerdmans, 2001.

Lowell, James Russell. "Love." In *The Poetical Works of James Russell Lowell in Four Volumes*, 1:22. Cambridge, MA: Riverside, 1890.

Mathewes-Green, Frederica. "Matters of Opinion: Men Behaving Justly." *Christianity Today*. November 17, 1997. Accessed February 26, 2014. http://www.christianitytoday.com/ct/1997/november17/7td045.html?paging=off.

McDowell, Josh. "What's the Difference between Love and Infatuation?" *Josh.org*. Accessed February 26, 2014. http://www.josh.org/resources/find-help/answers-for-teens/love/whats-the-difference-between-love-and-infatuation/.

McRae, William J. *Preparing for Your Marriage*. Grand Rapids: Zondervan, 1980.

Michael, Robert, John Gagnon, Edward Laumann, and Gina Kolata. *Sex in America: A Definitive Survey*. Boston: Little, Brown and Co., 1994.

Nelson, Tommy. *The Book of Romance: What Solomon Says about Love, Sex, and Intimacy*. Nashville: Thomas Nelson, 1998.

O'Donnell, Douglas Sean. *The Song of Solomon: An Invitation to Intimacy.* Preaching the Word. Wheaton: Crossway, 2012.

Patterson, Paige. *Song of Solomon.* Everyman's Bible Commentary. Chicago: Moody, 1986.

Penner, Clifford, and Joyce Penner. *Sexual Fulfillment in Marriage: A Multimedia Learning Kit.* Pasadena, CA: Family Concern, 1977.

Peterson, Karen S. "Sweet Nothings Help Marriages Stick." *USA Today.* March 30, 2000.

———. "To Fight Stress, Women Talk, Men Walk." *USA Today.* August 7, 1999.

Phillips, John. *Exploring the Song of Solomon.* Neptune, NJ: Loizeaux Brothers, 1984.

Pierson, Marie. "Nourishing Your Love." *Virtue.* N.d.

Piper, John. *This Momentary Marriage: A Parable of Permanence.* Wheaton: Crossway, 2009.

Regnerus, Mark, and Jeremy Uecker. *Premarital Sex in America: How Young Americans Meet, Mate, and Think about Marrying.* New York: Oxford University Press, 2011.

Rigstad, Dennis. "Is It Love or Lust?" *Psychology for Living.* February 1988.

Roberts, Sam. "Divorce after 50 Grows More Common." *New York Times.* September 20, 2013.

Rubenstein, Carin. "The Modern Art of Courtly Love." *Psychology Today* 17/7 (1983): 43–49.

Ryle, J. C. *Expository Thoughts on the Gospel of Mark.* Grand Rapids: Zondervan, 1951.

Saucy, Robert L. *The Church in God's Program.* Chicago: Moody, 1972.

Schwab, George M. "Song of Songs." In *The Expositor's Bible Commentary, Revised Edition,* edited by Tremper Longman III and David E. Garland, 6:367–431. Grand Rapids, MI: Zondervan, 2008.

Smalley, Gary, and John Trent. *The Gift of the Blessing.* Nashville: Thomas Nelson, 1993.

Snaith, John G. *The Song of Songs.* New Century Bible Commentary. Grand Rapids: Eerdmans, 1993.

Sommers, Christina Hoff. "Being a Man: Harvey Mansfield Ponders the Male of the Species." *The Weekly Standard,* April 4, 2006. Accessed January 15, 2013. http://www.weeklystandard.com/Content/Public/Articles/000/000/012/041bqgoo.asp#.

Spurgeon, C. H. *The Most Holy Place.* Ross-shire, Great Britain: Christian Focus, 1996.

————. "Apostolic Exhortation." Sermon preached at Metropolitan Tabernacle, London, April 1868. Accessed February 6, 2014. http://www.spurgeon.org/sermons/0804.htm.

Stack, Peggy Fletcher. "What They Didn't Teach You about Sex in Sunday School." *Religious News Service.* October 13, 2000.

Stephens, Steve, "37 Things to Say to your Spouse." In *Stories for the Heart,* compiled by Alice Gray, 190–91. Sisters, OR: Multnomah, 1996.

————. "27 Things Not to Say to Your Spouse." In *Stories for the Heart,* compiled by Alice Gray, 188–89. Sisters, OR: Multnomah, 1996.

Turnbull, Bob, and Yvonne Turnball. "What Your Wife Really Wants." *The Peaceful Mom* (blog). Accessed February 6, 2014. http://the-peacefulmom.com/wp-content/uploads/2011/10/What-Your-Wife-Really-Wants-1.pdf.

————. "What Your Husband Really Wants." *The Peaceful Mom* (blog). AccessedFebruary6,2014.http://thepeacefulmom.com/wp-content/uploads/2011/10/WHAT-YOUR-HUSBAND-REALLY-WANTS.pdf.

Van Buren, Abigail. "And You Wonder Why It Didn't Last." *Find The Power.* Accessed February 26, 2014. http://www.findthepower.net/CP/IL/PostNewABC2_I.php?IL=ON&SeeAlso=MOTIVE.

Walsh, Julie. "Who's Lighting the Fire? A Look into the Importance of Initiating Sex." *WebMD Medical News.* March 16, 2000. Accessed February20,2014.http://www.webmd.com/sex-relationships/features/whos-lighting-fire.

"What Happy Couples Say about Sex." *Readers' Digest.* February 1989, 13–16.

Weaver, Joanna. "25 Ways to Love Your Lover." *Posted Johnhansen.tv* (blog). Accessed February 26, 2014. http://johnhansen.tv/stuff/2011/2/12/25-ways-to-love-your-lover.html.

Webb, Barry G. *Five Festal Garments: Christian Reflections on the Song of Songs, Ruth, Lamentations, Ecclesiastes, and Esther.* New Studies in Biblical Theology. Downers Grove: InterVarsity, 2000.

Westcott, Brooke Foss. *Saint Paul's Epistle to the Ephesians.* Grand Rapids, MI: Eerdmans, 1952.

Wright, H. Norman. "The 8-Cow Wife." *Marriage.* Volume 30, issue 3, May/June 2000, 8–11.

Yamauchi, Edwin M. "Cultural Aspects of Marriage in the Ancient World." *Bibliotheca Sacra* 135(1978): 241–52.

SCRIPTURE INDEX